THE AESTHETICS OF

DISAPPEARANCE

SEMIOTEXT(E) FOREIGN AGENTS SERIES

© 2009 by Semiotext(e)
Originally published in 1980 as *Esthétique de la disparition* by Éditions
Balland, Paris.

Published by Semiotext(e)
2007 Wilshire Blvd., Suite 427, Los Angeles, CA 90057
www.semiotexte.com

Special thanks to John David Ebert, Jonathan Isaac, Steve Jones, Paul Virilio
and Jordan Zinovich.

Covert Art: James Welling, #002, 2005
C-Print mounted to Plexiglas. Print: 34 X 27 inches.
©James Welling. Courtesy the artist and David Zwirner, New York.

Back Cover Photography by Sylvère Lotringer
Design by Hedi El Kholti

ISBN: 978-1-58435-074-3
Distributed by The MIT Press, Cambridge, Mass. and London, England
Printed in the United States of America

10 9 8 7 6 5 4 3

THE AESTHETICS OF

DISAPPEARANCE

Paul Virilio

Introduction by Jonathan Crary

Translated by Philip Beitchman

<e>

Contents

Introduction by Jonathan Crary 9

Part 1 19

Part 2 51

Part 3 85

Part 4 109

Notes 123

Jonathan Crary

Introduction to *Aesthetics of Disappearance*

Nearly three decades have passed since the publication of *Esthétique de la disparition* in 1980. The immediate context in which it was written was the late 1970s, now to all of us like a foreign country. This was the bipolar world of the Cold War; globalization (though very much occurring at the time) was not on everyone's mind; most people still used typewriters, not yet word processors; even the VCR had not yet become a pervasive consumer item; the Internet was years away from widespread implantation; and the late 20th-century catastrophes of the Balkans, Rwanda, the Persian Gulf and elsewhere were hardly foreseeable from within the 1970s balance of terror management system.

So how now, in the early 21st century, does this remarkable Paul Virilio text resonate? Perhaps at the least, its rereading can help correct some of the wrongheaded characterizations of his work that have accumulated in these intervening years. This text in particular makes plain what has been obvious to any careful reader of Virilio all along: he never was or is a critic/historian of media or a philosopher of technology in the way these labels might apply to figures as disparate as Ellul, McLuhan, Kittler or Stiegler. Of course his work has been uniquely valuable to anyone interested in these areas but Virilio's guiding preoccupations lie elsewhere. To use quasi-Kantian terms, it is more accurate to see his work as a relentless examination of the conditions which make experience possible. But it is hard to imagine a more sweeping abandonment of the universalizing presumptions of Kant's critique than the arguments of *The Aesthetics of Disappearance* (the irony of the title is notable in this respect). For Kant, the essential role of time was to coherently unite all the elements of knowledge by establishing a relation between thought and perception. That is, time was the necessary condition of any particular experience we have; time is what makes perception possible and intelligible. Virilio's project is to uncover the role of time in the multiple and abyssal de-linkages of perception and its possible objects. But he is hardly interested in developing a new philosophical account of time, in the footsteps of Bergson, Husserl, Heidegger or others. His stance is more Nietzschean in his articulation of time as irreducibly plural, discontinuous, non-homogenous, and reversible. As they were for Foucault in the 1970s, questions of time for Virilio are of interest primarily as the consequences of a given field of forces and effects. Thus both Foucault and Virilio were aligned, at least for a time, in their related concern with how individual and collective experience is shaped territorially by strategic relations of power.

It should be stressed that Virilio is hardly proposing that prior to the industrial revolution, humans had some more "natural" relation to temporality. At the heart of *Aesthetics of Disappearance* is the insistence that experience as duration has always been constituted as de-synchronized and fractured. This is the importance of his thematic of "picnolepsy," his de-pathologizing of the epileptic "petit mal." Perhaps he could have chosen another, equally effective illustration to make his point, for he is writing not from the standpoint of medical physiology but from that of the phenomenology of perception, even if his project diverges from most of the work done within the framework of the latter (including by Merleau-Ponty). Virilio's "phenomenology" (for which he would substitute the term "logistics") discovers perception to be made of breaks, absences, dislocations as well as by the capacity to produce patchworks of various contingent worlds.

Historically, there have been a wide range of ways in which societies have responded to the vagaries and inconsistencies of perception, for example, the many pre-modern privilegings of states of trance, possession, or daydream and the ways these states were creatively integrated into collective life. But Virilio implies that wherever forms of logical or rational thought have dominated, especially in the West, the vacancies and absences in perception are assimilated and de-singularized into a homogenized and potentially controllable texture of events. The goal of reason, he says, is "to redistribute methodically the occasional eliminations of picnolepsy...to deny to particular absences any active value."

Thus Virilio is demonstrating that an individual is never organically situated in some *a priori* river of time but rather that history has always been a matter of shifting arrangements and techniques through which provisional systems of time are produced. The problem of speed, for example, with which Virilio's thought is popularly identified, is hardly something specific to recent modernity. Every historical epoch, whether the Roman empire or the Napoleonic, is understandable in terms of speeds, forms of motion and stasis, and their possibilities of modification. The last 150 years are different only in the rate of change and the intensified accumulation of overlapping technologies and networks. Surely this much broader historical vision of speed and territory was part of what appealed to Deleuze and Guattari in their use of Virilio's ideas in *Mille Plateaux* (also published in 1980). At the same time, the *Aesthetics of Disappearance* affirms that speeds are produced not just by what are commonly thought of as technologies, but by vectors and itineraries of many kinds.

One of the decisive elements of the present text (and of course in much of Virilio's writing) is cinema and the cinematic. In these pages, cinema is important as one of the most pervasive ways in which the absences in human perceptions are both supplemented and redeployed by an external production of speed, displacement and luminosity. Virilio certainly does not underestimate the consequential significance of the invention of the cinematograph in the 1890s but his sense of the cinematic is far more expansive and suggestive than most perspectives on film history. Components of a cinematic machine have been in use over many centuries: forms of projection, moving images, immobile voyages, and visionary illuminations. No doubt the extraordinary fascination on the part of artists and film makers with Joan of Arc in the first half of the 20th century was a dim recognition of a kindred picnoleptic in the 15th century who watched her own "home movies" as a girl in the countryside. But the various cinemas of the long pre-cinematic are in no sense anticipating their teleological assembly and unification at the hands of the Lumiere brothers. As is clear from the our 21st century vantage point, the cinematograph was itself only a temporary aggregate of parts that have been discarded or subsequently recombined into other proliferating "vision machines."

As Virilio wrote in the late 1970s, psychoanalytic film theory was exploring the similarities between the movie spectator and the sleeper/dreamer. But unlike Metz and others, Virilio saw the cinematic as part of a much wider breakdown of the boundaries between sleeping and waking, between the real and dreaming. Like Deleuze, Virilio understood cinema as part of a crisis of belief, in which we no longer believe in the world. This loss of faith is inseparable from an on-going incapacitation and neutralization of vision. Over the last century vision has increasingly been denied any hierarchy of objects within which the important could be distinguished from the trivial, as figure might be isolated from ground. Without these distinctions vision becomes a derelict and uninflected mode of reception and inertia, incapable of seeing. Along with its motorized speeds, cinema and an array of other luminous screens announce the installation of permanent day that by now has become part of the 24/7 globalized present we all inhabit. Virilio in the late 1970s was already specifying the broad inscription of human life into a homogenous global time without pauses or rest, a milieu of continuous functioning, of countless operations that are effectively ceaseless. 24/7 is a time that no longer passes, beyond clock time, beyond any measure of lived human duration.

This is why Virilio's epiphanic account of Howard Hughes remains so compelling. Hughes stands as a person-ification of the overlapping effects of speed (his obsession with flight) and light (his control of the movie industry) but also in his later life as bleak evidence of the unintended con-sequences of these new configurations. Hughes' atemporal isolation as he watched and rewatched screenings of *Ice Station Zebra* prefigures all the forms of timelessness and non-stop digital management of our own micro-programmed and atopic lives. In Virilio's words, "the internment of bodies is no longer in the cinematic cell of travel but in a cell outside of time, which would be an electronic terminal where we'd leave it up to the instruments to organize our most intimate vital rhythms, without ever changing position ourselves, the authority of electronic automatism reducing our will to zero."

The world as we see it is passing.

— Paul of Tarsus

1

The lapse occurs frequently at breakfast and the cup dropped and overturned on the table is its well-known consequence. The absence lasts a few seconds; its beginning and its end are sudden. The senses function, but are nevertheless closed to external impressions. The return being just as sudden as the departure, the arrested word and action are picked up again where they have been interrupted. Conscious time comes together again automatically, forming a continuous time without apparent breaks. For these absences, which can be quite numerous, hundreds every day most often pass completely unnoticed by others around—we'll be using the word "picnolepsy" (from the Greek, *picnos*: frequent).[1] However, for the picnoleptic, nothing really has happened, the missing time never existed. At each crisis, without realizing it, a little of his or her life simply escaped.

Children are the most frequent victims, and the situation of the young picnoleptic quickly becomes intolerable. People want to persuade him of the existence of events that he has not seen, though they effectively happened in his presence; and as he can't be made to believe in them he's considered a half-wit and convicted of lies and dissimulation. Secretly bewildered and tormented by the demands of those near him, in order to find information he needs constantly to stretch the limits of his memory. When we place a bouquet under the eyes of the young picnoleptic and we ask him to draw it, he draws not only the bouquet but also the person who is supposed to have placed it in the vase, and even the field of flowers where it was possibly gathered. There is a tendency to patch up sequences, readjusting their contours to make equivalents out of what the picnoleptic has seen and what he has not been able to see, what he remembers and what, evidently, he cannot remember and that it is necessary to invent, to recreate, in order to lend verisimilitude to his *discursus*.[2] Later, the young picnoleptic will himself be inclined to doubt the knowledge and concordant evidence of those around him; everything certain will become suspect. He'll be inclined to believe (like Sextus Empiricus) that nothing really exists; that even if there is existence, it cannot be described; and that even if it could be described, it could certainly not be communicated or explained to others.

Around 1913 Walter Benjamin noted: "We know nothing of woman's culture, just as we know nothing of the culture of the young." But the trivial parallel—woman/child—can find itself justified in the observation of Doctor Richet: "Hysterical women are more feminine than other women. They have transitory and vivid feelings, mobile and brilliant imaginations and, with it all, the inability to control, through reason and judgment, these feelings and imaginations."[3]

Just like women, children assimilate vaguely game and disobedience. Childhood society surrounds its activities with a veritable secret strategy, tolerating with difficulty the gaze of adults, before whom they sense an inexplicable shame. The uncertainty of the game renews picnoleptic uncertainty, its character at once surprising and reprehensible. The little child who, after awaking with difficulty, is absent without knowing it every morning and involuntarily upsets his cup, is treated as awkward, reprimanded and finally punished.

I'll transcribe here, from memory, the statements made by the photographer Jacques-Henri Lartigue, in the course of a recent interview:

Q: You've talked to me just now of a trap for vision, something like that, is that your camera?

A: No, not at all. It's before, something I did when I was little. When I half-closed my eyes, there remained only a narrow slot through which I regarded intensely what I wanted to see. Then I turned around three times and thought, by so doing, I'd caught—trapped—what I was looking at, so as to be able to keep indefinitely not only what I had seen, but also the colors, the noises. Of course, in the long run, I realized that my invention wasn't working. It's then only that I turned to technical tools for facilitating it.

Another photographer has written that his first dark-room was his room when he was a child and his first lens was the luminous crack of his closed shutter. But the remarkable thing with the little Lartigue is that he's assimilated his own body to the camera, the room of his eye to a technical tool, the time of the exposure to turning himself around three times.

He perceives a certain pattern there, and also sees that this pattern can be restored by a certain *savoir faire*. The child Lartigue has thereby stayed in the same place, and is, nevertheless, absent. Owing to an acceleration of speed, he's succeeded in modifying his actual duration; he's taken it off from his lived time. To stop "registering" it was enough for him to provoke a body-acceleration, a dizziness that reduced his environment to a sort of luminous chaos. But with each return, when he tried to resolve the image, he obtained only a clearer perception of its variations.

Child-society frequently utilizes turnings, spinning around, disequilibrium. It looks for sensations of vertigo and disorder as sources of pleasure.

The author of the famous comic strip *Luc Bradefer* uses the same method to transport his hero's vehicle through time: by spinning on itself like a top, the "Chronosphere" escapes from present appearances.

In another game, the first child places his nose against the wall, turning his back on his partners, who all stay a certain distance away on a starting line. He hits the wall three times before turning suddenly on his partners. During this short period of time, the others should advance toward him; then, when he turns around, they assume an immobile position. Anyone caught moving by the first child is eliminated from the game. Whoever succeeds in reaching the wall without being detected by the first child has won, and replaces him. As in the scansion of the game of handball, projected always higher and faster against the earth, a wall, or toward a partner, it seems that it is less the object that is being thrown and caught with agility than its image, projected, enlarged, deformed or erased by the player turning on himself. We may think here of the "leap" of Mandelbrot's skein of thread[4]—the numerical result (from zero to many dimensions), depending on the rapports of distance between the observed and the observing, or what separates them.

When asked how, at an advanced age, he was able to keep his youthful look, Lartigue answered simply that he knew how to give orders to his body. The disenchantment, the loss of power over himself that obliged him to have recourse to technical prostheses (photography, easel painting, rapid vehicles…) have not entirely abolished the demands on his own body that he made as a child.

But we now know that unequal aging of cellular tissues begins at a very early age, and the crystalline lens of the eye is affected precociously since breadth of accommodation declines after the age of eight until about fifty, when we become far-sighted. The nerve cells of the brain start their irreversible decline at age five. The child is already becoming a handicapped oldster; his recourse to prostheses here is really meant to be an artificial addition destined to replace or complete failing organs. The game then becomes the basic art; the contract on the aleatory is only the formulation of an essential question on the relative perception of the moving; *the pursuit of form is only a technical pursuit of time.* The game is neither naive nor funny. Begun by all from birth, it's the very austerity of its tools, its rules and its representations that paradoxically unleashes in the child pleasure and even passion: a few lines or signs traced ephemerally, a few characteristic numbers, some rocks or bones…

The basis of the game is the separation of the two extreme poles of the *seen* and the *unseen,* which is why its construction, the unanimity that pushes children to spontaneous acceptance of its rules, brings us back to the picnoleptic experience.

The more progress we make in the already ancient study of the *petit mal,* the more it appears to be widespread, diverse, and badly understood. In spite of lengthy polemics as to its kinship with epilepsy, with its uncertain diagnoses and with the crisis passing unperceived by those present as well as by the subject himself, it remains completely unknown by nearly everyone, and to the question: who is picnoleptic? we could possibly respond today: who isn't, or hasn't been?

So-defined as a mass phenomenon, picnolepsy comes to complement in the waking order the notion of *paradoxical sleep* (rapid-eye-movement sleep), which corresponds to the phase of deepest dreaming. So our conscious life—which we already believe would be inconceivable without dreams—is just as difficult to imagine without *a state of paradoxical waking* (rapid waking).

"Film what doesn't exist," the Anglo-Saxon special effects masters still say, which is basically inexact: what they are filming certainly does exist, in one manner or another. It's the speed at which they film that doesn't exist, and is the pure invention of the cinematographic motor. About these special effects—or "trick photography," hardly an academic phrase—Méliès liked to joke, "The trick, intelligently applied, today allows us to *make visible the supernatural, the imaginary, even the impossible.*"

The great producers of the epoch recognized that by wresting cinema *from the realism* of "outdoor subjects" that would quickly have bored audiences, Méliès had actually made it possible for film to remain realistic.[5]

As Méliès himself remarked, "I must say, to my great regret, the cheapest tricks have the greatest impact." It's useful to remember how he went about inventing that cheap trick which, according to him, the public found so appealing:

> "One day, when I was prosaically filming the Place de l'Opera, an obstruction of the apparatus that I was using produced an unexpected effect. I had to stop a minute to free the film and started up the machine again. During this time passersby, omnibuses, cars, had all changed places, of course. When I later projected the reattached film, I suddenly saw the Madeleine-Bastille Bus changed into a hearse, and

men changed into women. The trick-by-substitution, soon called the stop trick, had been invented, and two days later I performed the first metamorphosis of men into women."

Technical chance had created the desynchronizing circumstances of the picnoleptic crisis and Méliès—delegating to the motor the power of breaking the methodical series of filmed instants—acted like a child, regluing sequences and so suppressing all apparent breaks in duration. Only here, the "black out" was so long that the *effect of reality* was radically modified.

"Successive images representing the various positions that a living being traveling at a certain speed has occupied in space over a series of instants."

This definition of chronophotography given by its inventor, the engineer Etienne Jules Marey,[6] is very close also to that "game against the wall" we've just been talking of. Furthermore, if Marey wants to explore movement, making of fugacity a "spectacle" is far from his intentions. Around 1880 the debate centered on the inability of the eye to capture the body-in-motion, everyone was wondering about the veracity of chronophotography, its scientific value—the very reality it conveys insofar as it makes the "unseen" visible, that is to say, a world-without-memory and of unstable dimensions.

If we notice Marey's subject of choice we perceive that he leans toward the observation of what seemed to him precisely the most uncontrollable thing formally: the flight of free flying birds, or of insects, the dynamics of fluids… but also the amplitude of movement and abnormal expressions in nervous maladies, *epilepsy*, for instance (subjects of photographic studies around 1876 at the hospital of Salpetrière).

Later, the illusionism of Méliès will no more aim to mislead us than the methodical rigor of a Claude Bernard disciple: one maintains a Cartesian discourse, "the senses mislead us," and the other invites us to recognize that "our illusions don't mislead us in always lying to us!" (La Fontaine). What science attempts to illuminate, "the non-seen of the lost moments," becomes with Méliès *the very basis of the production of appearance*, of his invention, what he shows of reality is what reacts continually to the absences of the reality which has passed.

It's their "in-between state" that makes these forms visible that he qualifies as "impossible, supernatural, marvelous." But Emile Cohl's earliest moving comic strips show even more clearly to what extent we are eager to perceive malleable forms, to introduce a perpetual anamorphosis in cinematic metamorphosis.

The pursuit of forms is only a pursuit of time, but if there are no stable forms, there are no forms at all. We might think that the domain of forms is similar to that of writing: If you see a deaf-mute expressing himself you notice that his mimicry, his actions are already drawings and you immediately think of the passage to writing as it is still taught in Japan, for example, with gestures performed by the professor for students to capture calligraphically. Likewise, if you're talking about cinematic anamorphosis, you might think of its pure representation which would be the shadow projected by the staff of the sundial. The passing of time is indicated, according to the season of the year, not only by the position but also by the invisible movement of the form of the shadow of the staff or of the triangle on the surface of the dial (longer, shorter, wider, etc.).

Furthermore, the hands of the clock will always produce a modification of the position, as invisible for the average eye as planetary movements; however, as in cinema, the anamorphosis properly speaking disappears in the motor of the clock, until this ensemble is in turn erased by the electronic display of hours and dates on the black screen where the *luminous emission* substitutes entirely for the original effect of the shadow.

Emphasizing motion more than form is, first of all, to change the roles of day and light. Here also Marey is informative. With him light is no longer the sun's "lighting up the stable masses of assembled volumes whose shadows alone are in movement." Marey gives light instead another role; he makes it leading lady in the chrono-photographic universe: if he observes the movement of a liquid it's due to the artifice of shiny pastilles in suspension; for animal movement he uses little metallicized strips etc.

With him the effect of the real becomes that of the readiness of a luminous emission; what is given to see is due to the phenomena of acceleration and deceleration in every respect identifiable with intensities of light. He treats light like a shadow of time.

We notice generally a spontaneous disappearance of picnoleptic crises at the end of childhood (*infans*, the non-speaker). Absence ceases therefore to have a prime effect on consciousness when adult life begins (we may be reminded here of the importance of the endocrinal factor in the domain of epilepsy and also of the particular role of the pituitary and hypothalamus in sexual activity and sleep…).

Along with organic aging, this is also the loss of savoir-faire and juvenile capacities, the desynchronization effect stops being mastered and enacted, as with the young Lartigue playing with time, or using it as a system of invention and personal protection—photosensitive subjects show great interest for the causes inducing their crises and frequently resort to absence mechanisms as a defense-reaction against unpleasant demands or trains of thought (Pond).

The relation to dimensions changes drastically. What happens has nothing to do with metaphors of the "images of time" style; it is something like what Rilke's phrase meant in the most literal sense: "What happens is so far ahead of what we think, of our intentions, that we can never catch up with it and never really know its true appearance." One of the most widespread problems of puberty is the adolescent's discovery of his own body as strange and estranged, a discovery felt as a mutilation, a reason to despair.

It's the age of "bad habits" (drugs, masturbation, alcohol), which are merely efforts at reconciliation with yourself, attenuated adaptations of the vanished epileptic process. This is also the age, nowadays, of the intemperate utilization of technical prostheses of mediatization (radio, motorcycle, photo, hi-fi, etc.). The settled man seems to forget entirely the child he was and *believed eternal* (E.A. Poe); he's entered, in fact, as Rilke suggests, another kind of absence to the world. "The luxuriance and illusion of instant paradises, based on roads, cities, the sword,"[7] to which the Judeo-Christian tradition opposes a new departure toward a "desert of *uncertainties*" (Abraham), lost times, green paradises where only adults who have become children again may enter.

In Ecciesiastes *what is the essential* is lacking; with the New Testament *the lack is the essential*; the Beatitudes speak of a poverty of spirit that somehow could be opposed to the *wealth of moments*, to this hypothetical conscious hoarding proposed by Bachelard, to this fear "of mini-max equilibrium by exhaustion of the stakes based on a knowledge (information, if you will), whose treasure (which is language's treasure of possible enunciations) becomes inexhaustible" (J.F. Lyotard). Images of the vigilant society, striking equal hours for everyone.

At the Arch of Triumph Award, a journalist wittily asked of the president: "Is betting part of leisure?" The president was careful not to answer this question that pretended to assimilate lottery techniques to this *culture of leisure* proposed for more than a century to the working population as inestimable recompense for its efforts. Replying would be to admit that progress has pushed our hyper-anticipatory and predictive society toward a simple *culture of chance*, a contract on the aleatory.

In new Roman circuses at Las Vegas, they bet on any and everything, in the game rooms and even in the hospitals— even on death. A nurse working at the Sunrise Hospital invented, for the amusement of the personnel, a "casino of death" where you bet on the moment the patient will die. Soon everyone started playing: doctors, nurses, cleaning ladies; from a few dollars the stakes went up to hundreds... soon there weren't enough people dying. What follows is easy enough to imagine.

The basic recreation of childhood, lowered to the level of trivial excitement, remains nonetheless a derivative of picnoleptic auto-induction, the dissimulation of one or several elements of a totality in relation to an adversary who is one only because of differences in perception dependent on time and appearances that escape under our very eyes, artificially creating this inexplicable exaltation where "each believes he is finding his real nature in a truth which he would be the only one to know."

Furthermore, number-games, like lotto or the lottery, with their disproportionate winnings, connote disobedience to society's laws, exemption from taxes, immediate redress-ment of poverty...[8]

"No power doubles or precedes the will; the will itself is this power," wrote Vladimir Jankelevitch. If you admit that picnolepsy is a phenomenon that effects the conscious dura-tion of everyone—beyond Good and Evil, a *petit mal,* as it used to be called—the meditation on Time would not only be the preliminary job delegated to the metaphysician;

relieved today by a few omnipotent technocrats, anyone would now live a duration which would be his own and no one else's, by way of what you could call *the uncertain conformation of his intermediate times*, and the picnoleptic onset would be something that could make us think of human liberty, in the sense that it would be a latitude given to each man to invent his own relations to time and therefore a kind of will and power for minds, none of which, "mysteriously, can think of himself as being any lower than anyone else" (E. A. Poe).

With Bergsonian chrono-tropisms you could already imagine "different rhythms of duration that, slower or faster, would measure the degree of tension or of relaxation of consciousness and would establish their respective places in the series of beings." But here the very notion of rhythm implies a certain automatism, a symmetrical return of weak or strong terms superimposed on the experienced time of the subject. With the irregularity of the epileptic space, defined by surprise and an unpredictable variation of frequencies, it's no longer a matter of tension or attention, but of suspension pure and simple (by acceleration), disappearance and effective reappearance of the real, departure from duration.

To Descartes' sentence: "the mind is a thing that thinks" (that is, in stable and commonly visible forms), Bergson retorted: "The mind is a thing that lasts..." The paradoxical state of waking would finally make them both agree: it's our duration that thinks, the first product of consciousness would be its own speed in its distance of time, speed would be the causal idea, the idea before the idea.[9]

Even if we talk about the solitude of power as an established fact, no one really thinks of questioning this autism conferred inevitably by the function of command—which means that, as Balzac has it, "all power will be secret or will not be, since all *visible* strength is threatened."

This reflection radically opposes the extreme caducity of the world as we perceive it to the creative force of the unseen, the power of absence to that of the dream itself. Any man that seeks power isolates himself and tends naturally to exclude himself from the *dimensions* of the others, all techniques meant to unleash forces are techniques of disappearance (the epileptic constitution of the great conquerors, Alexander, Caesar, Hannibal, etc., is well known).

In his *Citizen Kane*, Orson Welles ignores the Freudian elements that American directors ordinarily used and designates the mysterious sled Rosebud as the apparently trivial motive for the rise to power of his hero, the key and the conclusion of the fate of this pitiless man, a little vehicle able to delight its young passenger while sliding at top speed through a snowscape.[10] After this fictive biography of William Randolph Hearst calling out to Rosebud for help in his agony, there comes Howard Hughes' real destiny. The life of this billionaire seems made of two distinct parts, first a public existence, and then—from age 47 and from then on for 24 years—a hidden life. The first part of Hughes' life could pass for a programming of behavior by dream and desire: he wanted to become the richest, the greatest aviator, the most important producer in the world, and he succeeded everywhere ostentatiously; overexposing his person, avid for publicity, for years he inundates the Western press with his image, with tales of his records or conquests of women.

Then, Howard Hughes disappears. He is in hiding until his death. The journalist James Phelan, who followed the billionaire's whole career, wonders about him:[11] "why did he allow himself to become *a man who couldn't stand being seen*? What was he looking for beyond the simple desire for acquisition?"

Master of an incomparable fortune, of a considerable technical and industrial achievement, the only purpose of his wealth, finally, was to purchase total reclusion in a dark room where he lived nude, covered with bedsores, emaciated and destitute on a pallet. Phelan concludes: what Hughes was accumulating was not money, but power.

One day, Phelan recounts, a man disguised as Mickey Mouse presented himself at the Bayshore Inn and said he had a gift for Mr. Hughes. He belonged to the Disney parade on a publicity tour, and they wanted to offer a "Mickey Mouse Watch" to Hughes with this inscription: "Legendary heros must constantly play cat-and-mouse with their public so that it will continue to believe in them, so you'll surely, once in awhile, want to know the time of day?"

Now it was notoriously well known that Hughes refused absolutely to wear a watch, all the while calling himself the *Master of Time*, which for him certainly had a precise meaning, close perhaps to Rilke's definition: to be all-powerful, to win in the game of life is to create a dichotomy between the marks of his own personal time and those of astronomical time, so as to master whatever happens and fulfill immediately what is in the offing.

Destitute billionaire, Hughes' only effort is to fake the speed of his destiny, to make his style of life a style of speed. He seems far more contemporary than Citizen Kane, emperor agonizing in his museum palace, buried in the ruins of his material goods, the baroque abundance of his collections.

For Hughes, on the other hand, *to be is not to inhabit*;[12] polytropos, like Homer's Ulysses, not occupying only one place, he desires not to be identifiable, but especially to identify with nothing. "He is no one because he wants to be no one and to be no one you have to be everywhere and nowhere." This taste for ubiquitous absence he'll quench, first through his use of various technical media, in surpassing what was then the most prestigious speed record: the 14th of July, 1938, his Lockheed-Cyclone having flown around the world "in a great circular arc," lands at Floyd Bennett Field where he had taken off on July 10th. Then he guides his plane into the hangar *to the exact point he left from.* It isn't long before Hughes recognizes that *his desire for movement is only desire of inertia, desire to see arrive what is left behind.*

Soon his only link to the world will be the telephone. Like Chateaubriand, *he locks into a narrow space his life-long hopes.* The rooms he wants to be in now are narrow and all alike, even if they are worlds apart. Not only does he thereby eliminate the impression of going from one place to another (as in the empty loop of the world record), but above all each place was such as he could have expected it to be. The windows were all shaded and the sunlight could no more penetrate these dark rooms than the unanticipated image of a different landscape.

Suppressing all uncertainty, Hughes could believe himself everywhere and nowhere, yesterday and tomorrow, since all points of reference to astronomical space or time were eliminated. At the foot of the bed where he was lying was, however, an artificial window, a movie screen. At the head there was a projector and alongside it, within reach, the controls that allowed him to project his films, always the same, eating indefinitely from the same plate.

We find here what we've always taken as a metaphor of vision, the Socratic myth of the cave (dark room), "where those (who have been first in everything) must be brought to their term, forcing them to face the light-giving source... to contemplate the real which is the invisible..."

Hughes wanted so much to be nowhere that he could no longer stand to be visible for others and if he supported, at great expense, a harem, he never went near his protégées, it was enough to know he had the power of going there and that the young women whose pictures he had were awaiting his arrival.

It was the same with his planes and cars, parked here and there, unused for years, exposed to the weather at sundry airports. He always bought the same model of Chevrolet because he thought this particular model was especially banal.

He treated his business like his women, maverick of politics, corruptor of the American government and the CIA, playing with the world, until finally he collapsed into states approximating sleep, then death.

In his absolute impatience to see arrive what is left, Hughes—who his fellow countrymen will end up calling a "mystic"—became a kind of *technological monk*, and there is very little difference between the dark room at the top of the Desert Inn in Las Vegas and the retreat to the desert of the ancient hermits in search of the Eternal.

The Hebraic tradition manifests two kinds of lack, expressed by two deserts, emerging one from the other, *heart of everything, in its heart everything.* One is named *Shemama*, despair and destruction, and the other is *Midbar*, which is a desert not of dereliction but instead a field of uncertainty and effort. The *shemama* is, rather, polarity of the City-State (City of *Ur*—*Our*, light), its desert is the tragical one of laws, ideology, order, as opposed to what could have resulted from wandering.

Hughes' life, his deprivation of the present world, seem risen from the Anchorites, from those "inhuman mortifications" that the monks inflicted upon themselves, at the end of those eremitic lives where the "saint" seemed to recognize only madness and idiocy, in this double game of city-desert and desert-of-uncertainties—like Simeon of Emesis, who comes down from his solitude, he said, so as to *mock the world* (or to play with the world, as Hughes).

According to the chronicle, the desert had so tired him that he had attained *apatheia*, which may be translated as impassibility, and which will allow him to make a mockery of the city and its laws, by acting in it like an idiot. Always dressed in his monastic habit, he doesn't hesitate to lift his skirts in public: he's a regular at the brothel, he goes to church to disturb the liturgy. Multiplying reprehensible acts, he puts his autism to the test by acting in the city as if it were a desert and no one could see him.

Photosensitive inductor, the desert (its double aspect) is linked in every case to liberation from time: divine eternity for the Anchorite, State eternity for Caesar dreaming of turning the frontiers of his empire into a vast desert.

Christ—the inverse of Hughes—begins by a hidden life to end in public existence, confronting temptation at the juncture of these two modes, Satan offering him domination over nations (the *shemama*), as if assuming human power could only be evoked by the overview of a solitary expanse where other people are on the verge of invisibility.

The preacher in John Huston's film, *Wise Blood*, expresses this pretty clearly: "The Church of Christ without Christ is nothing but your own shadow, nothing but your reflection in a mirror."

The singer Amanda Lear eliminated mirrors from her apartment, replacing them with an integrated video circuit; and so the light of her image follows after her like the most intimate of companions (like her shadow, you could say). If the aging Castiglione had veiled the mirrors in her home to avoid witnessing the progress of her decrepitude, Amanda would not have to fear meeting her reflection, she'll just stop taping the images on the day of her choice and the screens will return her eternally young image, in an apartment where time would stop, the movable property of the living would no longer be distinct from immovable real estate. The means of communication would become a synthesizer capable of mixing body and field in her house, the video game becoming a way of playing indefinitely with everyday life, accomplishing Baudelaire's notion:

> "Countless layers of ideas, images, feelings have fallen successively on your brain as softly as light. It seems that each buries the preceding, but none has really perished."

In their intimate memoirs, erudite Germans at the beginning of the century loved to alternate methodically an account of their days and stories of their dreams, trying to create an equivalence between their waking states and oneiric universes. This style was an attempt to abrogate an abusive discrimination between waking and sleeping: "Sleepers are in separate worlds, the awake, in the same" (Heraclitus).

German artists, who are known for their epileptic constitution, usually blur the ideal of ordinary Reason as activation of the conscious man and censor of the real, pretension to a state of wakefulness (of sentinel), in a world given as common (proto-foundation of meaning). But if you admit that each one's time has been more or less patched together and that rapid waking is as paradoxical as the dream, the reality of the passing world could in no sense seem common, and "pure reason" would be only one of the numerous subterfuges of the picnoleptic scheme and of its *savoir-faire*—one of the sophistications that worried Bachelard:

"Applied rationalism which is only a philosophy at work, which wants to expand... haste of systematic thought, authoritarian propensity that no one questions..."

Oppressive work, accompanied from childhood on with heavy punishments, for no one is supposed to ignore Reason, as none is excused from knowing the law. To juvenile consciousness, always time's orphan, Reason supplies the *illusory recommencement of its foreign tale*, as operational language, it's the pitiful "I knew" of the child who has recited his lesson well and so escaped punishment.

The ideal of scientific observation would therefore be a sort of *controlled trance* or, better yet, a control of the speed of consciousness. And it would be first of all as a reconstitution of picnoleptic *savoir-faire* that it could be communicated and recognized as common by each and everyone.

In his book, *Magic, Reason, and Experience*,[13] G.E.R. Lloyd, wondering about the passage from prescientific to scientific phases in the ancient Greeks, calls our attention to the importance of the Hippocratic text on *the sacred malady* (epilepsy) which dates from the end of the fifth century or the beginning of the fourth century, B.C. The goal of the author was to show that this malady is no more sacred than any other, that we could find natural causes for it and therefore treat it otherwise than by incantations or the efficacy of amulets. But what seems interesting to us here is that the epileptic process finds itself at the center of what nineteenth century people regarded as the advent of the absolute dichotomy between the magical and the scientific.

However, the Hippocratic text can be understood otherwise. To show that the divine malady is naturally explicable is to say that the rational study of the real (the establishment of its laws and its models) can be perfectly substituted for the epileptic randomness, curing us completely of its uneven and, especially, unpredictable frequencies.

We should remember that the divine system is also, for the Ancient Greek, a system of events: "The Gods are events in motion," which explains well enough this indecisive attitude that contemporary scholars find naive and incompatible with the formation of the scientific spirit, an ideal of science without accuracy where the rational project is presented as an incomplete program, or better yet as a simple bet on the universe where "*the real is the invisible*" (Plato).

Heisenberg tells us of Einstein's irritation, rebelling at the idea of a God playing with dice. Bachelard thought that the original sin of reason was to have an origin. Paul of Tarsus said that "reason resembles death."

If Ambrose Paré qualifies epilepsy as *retention of feelings*, in other civilizations the attenuated adaptations of the epileptic process, just like the accomplishment of the sexual act, are called "little death," "quick death." For sleep we talk about the "death you come back from." Reason, compared to death, does nothing else but redistribute methodically the occasional eliminations of picnolepsy.

The rational study of the real is just like the movies; the *tabula rasa* is only a trick whose purpose is to deny particular absences any active value.

Little by little the rational hoarding, as an expectation of the advent of what is left and a factor of non-surprise, turns our contemporaries into these characters afflicted with fly-catcher memories where whole masses of useless facts are glued together (Conan Doyle)—which makes us judge them *inferior* to those computer screens, where, in actual fact, the information of a memory without gaps, failures, absence is displayed at very high speeds, so we think.

Pascal, himself interested in the construction of this kind of fly-catcher memory, but equally afflicted by massive crises, proceeds by introducing disorder into the order in which information appears.

"What's new is not the elements but the order in which they are arranged," he writes. Finally the discovery, the invention, that is, that which is without possible memory and therefore new, is the order in which he alone, Pascal, could put into relation those elements known to all and this in "finally making reason yield to feeling."[14] For he knows from experience that the faculty of feeling, that is the aesthetic emotion, is at the heart of the epileptic onset; epilepsy is provokable, it can be domesticated.

We can see here likewise the very cause of his famous wager on the existence of God, which he assimilates to a *savoir-faire*, to a theological transposition of the scientific hypothesis, comparable to the ancient Greeks' approach.

The crisis, *sudden thunder in a calm heaven*, is announced by the very beauty of the sky. The epileptic isn't necessarily looking for the crisis as a factor of pleasure, but he has been warned of its coming by a very special state of happiness, a juvenile exhilaration. "Sublime," says Dostoevski, "for that moment you'd give your whole life!" He is literally "ravished," before returning, to be there again, often afflicted as he is by more or less severe lesions provoked by his fall or the sheer suddenness of the onset. The inexplicable enthusiasm precedes the accident, the shipwreck of the senses that of the body. But facilitating factors can also be of the order of distraction, the sleepiness provoked by the repetition of certain themes, or, on the contrary, by intense intellectual efforts, connected, for example, with the moment of invention, of basic discovery, as with Champollion, or with creative activity…

"At that moment I understood the meaning of that singular expression: there will no longer be time," says Dostoevski.

In photosensitive subjects the processes of autoinduction of absence are called autoerotic acts, with a sexual origin. As we have seen, at puberty picnolepsy interferes with the awakening of sexual activity. Here also absence is no stranger to invention, to the crystallization of the amorous image.

If antique statuary represents the sleeper in state of erection, the fact is that he is dreaming. We had to wait for the forties before scholars rediscovered this phenomenon, and later, the connections between paradoxical sleep and sexual activity in men and women.

Likewise the degree of love's power and of diurnal desire is a function of the invisible recall of the state of exaltation in paradoxical wakefulness.

Michelangelo writes: "Please tell me, O Love, if my eyes see (outside of me) true beauty or if I have it in me…" It is the curse of Psyche, where the external light instantaneously destroys the crystal of the love image, Eros flies, deserting the young woman as soon as she lights up her face. More simply, in the old ceremony of bundling, newly wed couples who often had never before met were advised to avoid immediate contacts and rather to sleep, that is, to dream, leaving it up to natural law to create the adhesion and "satisfaction" of the couple.

One might contrast this traditional method with the current hyper-wakefulness of sexual information and education, one result of which is to squash anything natural in sexual actions, psychoanalysts receiving nowadays visits from rationally educated young people who nevertheless don't know how "to go about it."

Which reminds us also of the sword placed between Tristan and Iseult while they're sleeping—to show us that the filter of passion has placed them in such a state of consciousness that the subterfuge of paradoxical sleep becomes useless. For them, love has created the equivalence of night and day, of rapid waking, of dream and soon of death.

We can multiply the examples and customs of dissimulation between future spouses right up to the idea of Catholic nuns wishing themselves married to Christ, who by his absolute invisibility is able to pass for a sort of absolute spouse, a new interior Eros, something that would facilitate another relation to time.

A mourning, an impression of profound unhappiness can, according to Bachelard, give us the feeling of the moment. They can, in any case, favor absence. We're afflicted and here we are visited by some tenacious sensation, affecting indifferently one of our organs of perception: in the olfactory domain, someone will sense, often for several days, a characteristic odor, connected to a far-off memory; another, seated in a garden, will see one flower among others become suddenly photogenic. The strange phenomenon lasts sometimes for a long while before everything seems ordinary again. You might think of Marcel Proust's reflection on the subject of the Marquise de Sévigne: "She does not present things in a logical, causal order, she first presents the illusion that strikes us." In the sequence of the arrival of information, Proust designates for us the stimulus of art as the fastest, since here nothing yields to sentiment, but on the contrary, everything begins with it.

In short, turned causal by its excessive speed, the sensation overtakes the logical order. Proust confirms the Sophist idea of *apate*, the suddenness of this possible entry into another logic "which dissolves the concepts of truth and illusion, of reality and appearance and which is given by the *kairos* that one might call 'opportunity.'"

What escapes from the universal and gives difference a context is the *epieikés*—that which pertains to a moment that is singular and, by definition, different.[15]

As for scientists, some today are dropping the pompous term of *basic research* for the more convenient *non-applied research*, research in which "that which is new, the discovery, obviously does not depend on chance, but on *surprise*" (P. Joliot).

The world is an illusion, and art is the presentation of the illusion of the world. Michelangelo detested, for example, the creating of an image imitating nature or liable to resemble a living model: "They paint in Flanders to fool our external vision... the beguilements of the world have robbed me of the time accorded me to worship God." Aging, he realized that the same duration can be utilized in diverse manners, or better yet, according to our art of seeing, the same time may serve to allow yourself to be fooled or to contemplate something other than what you think you're seeing (God, in this case, as Truth of the World).

In 1960 the painter, Magritte, responding to a questionnaire, expresses the same convictions:

Q: "Why is it that in some of your pictures bizarre objects appear, like the bilboquet?"

Magritte: "I don't think of a bilboquet as being bizarre. It's rather something very banal, as banal as a penholder, a key or the foot of a table. I never show bizarre or strange objects in my pictures... they are always familiar things, not bizarre but ordinary things are gathered and transformed in such a way that we're made to think that *there's something else of an unfamiliar nature that appears at the same time as familiar things.*"

To look at what you wouldn't look at, to hear what you wouldn't listen to, to be attentive to the banal, to the ordinary, to the infra-ordinary. To deny the ideal hierarchy of the crucial and the incidental, because there is no incidental, only dominant cultures that exile us from ourselves and others, a loss of meaning which is for us not only a *siesta* of consciousness but also a decline in existence.

In Europe, for more than a century now, many children have seen the Virgin *appear*, and the police and religious authorities have had to take down their testimony. As for me, I am struck by the sequence of circumstances that precedes the apparition proper and where the world begins to be seen by children as illusion of the world.

Particular selection of what is seen, recording of insignificant facts that gradually transforms the true objects into a sort of background against which another designation of meaning suddenly emerges, a background which would be already a kind of *dissolving view*, reminding us of the reflection of Paul of Tarsus (but he, also, on the road to Damascus, experienced a prolonged absence which effectively altered his notion of reality), all is calm, and yet: *this world as we see it is passing away.*

As for Magritte, above, it's a question of the recording of facts, or else of "camera shots," all you can see in the instant of the glance; isn't it only the imposture of the immediate, the untimely hijacking of a convoy of objective elements, among which operates the "shooting" of vision?

As the meteorologist explains: "the local level is always an uncertain objective, it's on the scale of the globe that we should envision the meteorological data, our weather's always somewhere else's weather and that's how the whole system fits together."

Bernadette Soubirous recounts:

"I heard a noise. Looking up I saw poplars beside the torrent and brambles in front of the cave quiver as if the wind was shaking them, but all around nothing moved and suddenly I saw something white... and this white was... a white girl... a white girl no bigger than me. She greeted me, bowing..."

Sometimes visual, but also olfactory, gustatory, auditory sensations are shared by several young witnesses. But here also the children experience the particular instants that precede the passage from the familiar to the unfamiliar.

At Salette, for example, two children who didn't know each other met by chance. Mélanie is a puny little servant, miserably poor, who's considered "withdrawn." Maximin is himself a young man with asthmatic heredity, considered as a madcap who spends most of his time running in the mountains after his goat but who can barely be trusted to watch over the herd. The day of the apparition, the two children, who have decided to watch their animals together, are overcome by a sudden desire to sleep, and, in fact, they both fall asleep, which was unusual for them. On awakening they are worried and set out to look for the herd they were supposed to be watching, but the animals are still in the same spot, they haven't moved. And suddenly, at the spot where the children were sleeping "a spinning globe of light, growing gradually, as if the sun had fallen there..."

Poor, scorned, considered as retarded, often asthmatic, these children will be, as a rule, deprived of apparitions and cured by puberty.

Bernadette Soubirous will say sadly: "You should refer to what I first said. I could have since forgotten and others also could have forgotten..."

"For that moment you'd give a whole lifetime." This is exactly what she does by hiding in a convent at Nevers where she dies at age 35.

The apparitions, therefore, have been like a repetition of those surprising moments that precede the epileptic absence, but the senses that stay awake succeed in perceiving an infra-ordinary reality.

Bernadette looked characteristically pale at that moment, "fine white muslin falling over her face," then she returned "rubbing her eyes and her face was alive with color once more."

But the apparent resemblance with epilepsy stops here, for Bernadette is able to function during the ecstasy, to move, to eat even, and, upon return, she will recall what happened. Nevertheless, as her visions multiply, the little girl feels the need to induce them by means of a personal ceremony, she acts nervous, which annoys certain witnesses, and, furthermore, she doesn't always succeed.

Later, when she leaves Lourdes to retire to the convent at Nevers, she stops at Bordeaux and "what she found most beautiful," she says, "is the aquarium of the Botanical Garden, seeing the little animals swimming in the presence of a crowd of fascinated children."

2

"Film is a new age for humanity."
— Marcel L'Herbier

Currently we're wondering about the excesses of methodological reason; we're discovering tardily "the vanity of theories taught before like eternal truths." This is bringing literary people to reconsider the transcendental themes or mystical materialism that were the bases of the new modes of life and production, in particular, in the United States during the 19th century. But to advocate abandoned ideas, to return to obsolete conceptions, is simply to exchange one error for another—or so they say.

This regression is guilty, unfortunately, of ignoring the *fait accompli* of technology. A technology detached from socio-economic or cultural preconceptions, desires to become the metaphor of the world, while envisioning itself as a revolution of consciousness—finally replacing the pseudo-state of rational wakefulness with an artificial condition of paradoxical wakefulness, while furnishing people with an assistance become subliminal.

Bernadette Soubirous is the worthy contemporary of the German idealists or the tenants of metapoetics, all able to see manifested "a world of inspirations, a magnificent procession festooned with disorderly and rhapsodic thoughts in the trembling of a leaf, the buzzing of a bee, or the vague odors of the forest…"

Of course it isn't a question of some revelation of magnetic sleep, but simply of looking for a unity of tone between the simple story of the young seers and the elaborate tales of the transcendental or symbolist poets. In fact, we notice in both cases a sort of *paraoptic aesthetics* of the real world, an unusual activity of the senses, usurping their functions by chance, from which rises, according to Edgar Poe, a sixth sense which would be *the moral perfection of the abstract human idea of time*:

> "This feeling of duration, lively, perfect, existing on its own, independent of any series of facts…"

With Poe (whose influence on Dostoevski, Kafka or Rilke is well known), there is not even any causal precedent or consequence; absence is mixed in with ruin, the progressing degeneration of a life-become-clinical. The lack is creator of an extrasensory perception (one might think of a blind man discerning the color of a flower from its fragrance or of Heinrich Heine, afflicted, he said, with musical pictography: a panoply of Chinese shadows leaping before his eyes with every Paganini flourish, as if the *different senses* had mistaken their outlets, as he tells it in his *Florentine Nights*).

Parapsychology renews the heritage of the mystical materialism of the nineteenth century, related in turn by current research in electronic matter. The main idea was to put into question the sensorial categories in a general way but especially from one individual to another, *to obtain an effect of sensorial mass.*

The enthusiasm of great materialistic states like Russia and America for research of this kind shouldn't surprise us. For the different powers to establish this transparency of consciousness through cohesion of sensations would be, in effect, an extraordinary advance. This new communion would no longer assume responsibility, as before, for our wills, our psychology, but instead our duration and therefore our causal ideas, the very essence of our personality.

"You don't have bodies, you are bodies!" was the cry once of Wilhelm Reich; to this, power and its techniques now respond: "You have no speed, you are speed!"

Already, in *Speed and Politics,*[1] I demonstrated how the modulation and manipulation of vectorial speeds (logistical police) were, in diverse military and revolutionary conflicts, the surest elements of mass cohesion in Europe and America. But at the same time I showed that the goal sought by power was less the invasion of territories, their occupation, than a sort of *recapitulation of the world* obtained by the ubiquity, the suddenness of military presence, a pure phenomenon of speed, a phenomenon on the way to the realization of its absolute essence.

However, in advancing too fast everything happens as if their own arsenal became the internal enemy of each of the protagonists. The very immediacy of the information risks creating the crisis immediately; soon dissuasion is necessary, the old war machine tending to be transformed into a total peace machine, of absolute pacification. To the ancient *kriegspiel*, war game for the world, succeeds a new game, exactly the way Hughes, the technological monk, replaces the game of monk-soldier or of "Saint-Simonian priest," by using unprecedented vectors.

Before the war of 1914 Doctor Gustav Lebon and many of his contemporaries were interested in mass psychology, this new kind of possession. He said about Germany's entry into war:

"Never was mental unification pushed farther, the individual soul was progressively destroyed to make of it a collective soul."

An editor of the *Lausanne Gazette* exclaims on his part: "You might say that a single brain thinks in millions of heads!" Lebon points out in his works the fateful consequences of psychological conformism, in particular in what is called basic research:

"Even isolated the German remains collective. The most individual book is signed by at least a dozen authors, which is deplorable because the wisest mind loses all perspective as soon as it submits to the law of collective influences... The certainty of facts, the incontestability of proofs, cannot exist for collective observation."

We in turn have come to know this frozenness, a veritable plague of collective conformity, and if it's now in fashion to criticize methodological reason, until now we have had almost no works addressing the repression of feeling in science in a group of scientists under its influence.

To the moralist formula: science without conscience can only be the ruin of the soul, might succeed something as simple as: science kills the conscience.

There was less to know in preceding centuries, and you'll notice that, paradoxically, knowledge then aimed at certainty and totality. The more knowledge grew the greater the unknown grew, we might conclude; or rather, the more information flashes by the more aware we are of its incomplete fragmentary nature.

We might also note that the great inventions are events in the order of consciousness more than in science. Archimedes, Newton, Einstein sense the principle of relativity while observing the flight of gulls over the sea—as a phenomenon of aesthetic surprise. All of this is effected, as they thought during the Renaissance, by the channel of sensation, Love & Reason being here only spatial-temporal dimensions given to the *imago*—units of measure.

The scientific spirit is the Apollo of classicism, remaining prisoner of his Promethean concept, it is this concept that has made it the unconditional ally of technique, this dream of reconstruction of man by his image. The West can no more tear itself from a science that is no more than the mirror of its intelligence than the singer Amanda Lear can detach herself from the reflection-in-stereo of her beauty even when the latter someday will have definitively disappeared.

Man, fascinated with himself, constructs his double, his intelligent specter, and entrusts the keeping of his knowledge to a reflection. We're still here in the domain of cinematic illusion, of the mirage of information precipitated on the computer screen what is given is exactly the information but not the sensation; it is *apatheia*, this scientific impassibility which makes it so that the more informed man is the more the desert of the world expands around him, the more the repetition of information (already known) upsets the stimuli of observation, overtaking them automatically, not only in memory (interior light) but first of all in the look, to the point that from now on it's the speed of light itself which limits the reading of information and the important thing in electronic information is no longer the storage but the display.

As the rational universe goes, so goes the effect of the real. Looking sideways, always sideways, rejecting fixity of attention, drifting from the object to the context, escaping from the source of habit, from the customary seems to have become impossible. The perceived world ceases to be deemed worthy of interest by dint of being theatrically exhumed, analyzed, purified by the pillagers of tombs.

If you leaf through a collection of photographs from the last century to today, you see in the succession of pictures not only the world in process of passing and succeeding itself, but especially you see the nature of the interest you can have in it disappear progressively: first of all, an interest essentially based on everyday anonymity, circulating in the ordinary then soon beyond, becoming tourist of the extraordinary, of ruins and events, the photograph tries to copy genre painting, is consecrated to travel, exoticism, to news items; all these poles of attraction disappear one after another.

In 1934 Walter Benjamin interrogates this photographic object, incapable of registering a barracks or a pile of garbage without transforming them:

"Transforming everything abject about poverty, it's transformed it also into an object of pleasure."

This stage of photographic art is today really *depassé* since photography, overcome by indifference, seems from now on incapable of finding something new to photograph. Already collective thought imposed by diverse media aimed at annihilating the originality of sensations, at dispensing with the presence in the world of people by furnishing them with a stock of information destined to program their memories. We now know that with the progress of electronics, we may envisage active prostheses of intelligence.

For about 20 years the neurosurgeon Delgado, one of the pioneers of the electronical phenomena of thought, has been treating and especially *tranquilizing* his patients with implants. Others are thinking of utilizing the "intelligence" of the computer as internal prosthesis:

"A miniscule pastille of silicon would give a person instantaneous knowledge of a foreign language or the theory of relativity…"

To offer man a memory that would no longer be his own these theoreticians think themselves able to justify this operation by employing, once more, the splitting effect of the old Promethean mirror:

"To take the step that separates man from a higher level… transforming the structure of the cerebral organ that has evolved very little for tens of thousands of years."

It is obvious that this step is simply inspired by the old military-political propaganda that is discussed above.

The speed of our cerebral automatisms is certainly the target aimed at in this electronic assumption, already foreshadowed by electroshock therapy, discovered in 1938, at the height of fascism, by the Italian psychiatrist Ugo Cerletti. We know that the method was used on pigs, at the Roman slaughterhouses. The animals were bled white during an epileptic coma provoked by electrocution. A simple decree that epileptics are never schizophrenics was enough for psychiatrists to oblige hundreds of thousands of patients to be submitted, after pigs, to electric shocks whose effects are still unknown… except in their use as punishment and, eventually, torture—as in Latin America, where electroshock treatment has become a common practice of the secret police.[2] We may think also of the treatments undergone by Hemingway in 1960, which *destroyed his skill as a writer at the same time as his memory.* One month later he committed suicide.

The confession by way of the political-military interrogation, extorted from the suspect by electroshock torture, is important also as a social or rather technico-social experience, a new effort towards transparency. Increasingly technical prostheses and medical prostheses tend to form new compounds destined for *pacification,* creation of a

> "consciousness without border and without bottom, total consciousness where the feverish *worry* of individual beings subsides…." (Empedocles)

Human prostheses, for about the last 40 years, have followed the extraordinary progress of biology, physics, electronics. During this brief period we've passed from quasi-inert anthropomorphic instruments to systems of active assistance *in the sensorial domain in particular,* a subliminal succour that ushers in a crisis of dimensions at the same time as one of representations.

With the emergence of the motor another sun has risen, changing vision radically: its light will not be long in changing life—due to the double projector, producing speed and propagating images (cinematic or cinematographic). Visibly, everything is alive, the disintegration of vision commences, preceding slightly that of matter and bodies, which was foreshadowed already with the first studies of the technology of least resistance (aerodynamics), where, with Marey, for example, speed and the elements combine to give form to the appearance of machines, anticipating the total recreation of their movement-field, the aeolian erosion doubled from now on by that of a speed that sculpts at the same time vehicle and landscape, while waiting to acclimate the passengers.

Although we can no more hide the speed of light than we can the sun with our hands, the disintegration of the transmission of the cinematographic image and of the transmission of cinematic bodies will be speedily accomplished, to such an extent that soon no one will be astonished at visual disturbances provoked by rapidity: the locomotive illusion will be thought of as the truth of vision, just as the illusions of optics will seem like those of life.

"Film is truth 24 times a second!" declares the director Jean-Luc Godard. The rhythm attained by Marey's chronophotographic motor was only truth 16 times a second.

In *The Art of Seeing* Aldous Huxley notes: "The wearing of black spectacles has become not merely common, but creditable... Black glasses have ceased to be the badge of the afflicted, and are now compatible with youth, smartness and sex appeal... In the Western world, millions of people now wear dark glasses, not merely on the beach, or when driving their cars, but even at dusk, or in the dim-lit corridors of public buildings... One can acquire an addiction to goggles, just as one can acquire an addiction to tobacco or alcohol... Animals get on very happily without goggles; so do primitive men... Why, then, do so many people in the contemporary world experience discomfort when exposed to light even of relatively low intensity?"

Huxley, without realizing it, gives the reason: animals and primitives don't expose themselves without good reason to the sun, any more than they affront the sun of the motors in cars, or at the movies. For Huxley, light remains *a priori* useful and natural, whereas, by experience, the wearer of dark glasses knows that the protectors-propagators of bodies and images are loaded weapons. He veils therefore prudently his retina and particularly the area of the *macula* with its little *fovea centralis*, the point of the sharpest sensations—and his fear of being surprised by the sudden onset of the image, the intense illumination of projectors and other vectors of the acceleration of the cinematic effect, is magnified when he finds himself in a place that is naturally dark or crepuscular. The wearer of dark glasses believes, like Alfred Jarry, *that light is active and shadow is passive, that light is not separated from shadow but penetrates it if only it is given the time.*[3]

In the process of vision, we should remember, objects are not given as *realities* and what is directly sensed by the eye, the primitive *matter of vision*, is, according to Doctor Broad, *something that has no substratum in itself.*

And so Huxley, under narcosis, receives when awakening a series of visual impressions that seem meaningless to him; he writes "they're not mine, they simply exist..."

Likewise, in practice, E.J. Marey understands that the acceleration of bodies, the fugacity of movement, as perceived by the vulgar eye, demand a guidance of vision disengaged from mnemonic traces. The whiteness of birds or that of horses, the brilliant strips pasted on the clothes of experimental subjects, make the body disappear in favor of an instantaneous blend of givens under the indirect light of motors and other propagators of the real. The heterogeneous succeeds the homogeneous, the aesthetics of the search supplants the search for an aesthetics, the aesthetics of disappearance renews the enterprise of appearance.

Reversible chronophotography, that is, cinema, *illusion imposed on the physiology of our organs of visual perception* (Alfred Fessard), oscillates, from the beginning, between the production of luminous, persisting impressions and the pure fascination that destroys the conscious perception of the spectator and conflicts with the natural functioning of the eye: "Fixity of the look directed at what we seriously think of as a single thing, for example, a colored spot, fixity that can last not much longer than a second without serious risk of seeing the subject fall into hypnotic ecstasy or into some other analogous pathological condition," writes Doctor Abraham Wolf.

Finally, with the cinematic accelerator, itself conceived as an active prosthesis, the measure of the world becomes that of the vector of movement, of the means of locomotion that de-synchronize time. When Marey reduces the movement of life to certain photogenic signs, he makes us penetrate into an unseen universe, where no form is given us since all forms fill a different time, stripped of mnemonic traces, already.

A few years ago an American television station came up with the idea of eliminating Christmas evening programs and replacing them with the transmission of continuous close up images of burning logs. By transforming in this way millions of receiving sets into "false fireplaces," these programmers intended to procure for the viewers a state as euphoric as that created by a variety show. The informal universe of light-in-motion produces, in effect, a characteristic torpor; fireplace blaze, logs, flames and flashes of joy leave us incapable of grasping the multitude of their transformations, for, at no moment do they present stable formations. It's strange to note that through a long series of coincidences and choices, the cinematographic industry thus continues the primordial work of its inventors.

We may notice in the first films of the Lumiére brothers the reflecting power of the white dresses worn (because they were in fashion, through concern with hygiene or fear of epidemics) by women and children. This was the time when, in fashion photography, the female models, who had shortly before been relieved of corsets, appear on white background so as finally to allow the lines of their bodies to be seen, while inversely, the mysterious star system, which becomes essential to the young spectacle industry, develops on the screen.

By definition the star must also be photogenic, actors of both sexes pile the rice-powder on their faces and bodies, dark haired women are said to be "less seductive," and the fashion of platinum hair, like that of lamé clothes, mirror-material of flashing metal, is destined to make of the star a formless being also, as diaphanous as if the light was pouring through her flesh; however the pellicle is really transparent and the star is only a specter of absorption proposed to the gaze of the spectator, *a ghost that you can interview*, said Michel Simon. The director Joseph von Sternberg described the actress' face as being a landscape, with its terrain, its lakes and valleys, over which the camera travels and that he, as director, is alone responsible for lighting up. As with Marey, the effect of the real is created by the luminous emission, the heteromorphy is born of the intensities of the lighting. But all of this seems natural enough, since the great moviemakers of the beginning of the century recognized the influence of the pioneers.

George Méliès' granddaughter, Madeleine Malthète-Méliès, says: "As a little girl I saw many movie people at the house that came to ask advice of grandfather: René Clair, Marcel Carné, Cavalcanti, Abel Gance, Walt Disney…"

Abel Gance loved quoting Napoleon: "To magnetize masses, you must above all talk to their eyes," and he affirms that *the future of the movies is a sun in each image*. A sun for visual truth, 24 times a second. Gance is of the opinion also that you have to *stuff the spectator's eye*; in his *Napoleon*, made around 1926–27, he multiplies the simultaneous images, up to 16 at a time, which, according to him, represents a threshold of vision that is very difficult to cross. In 1927 he's being consistent with himself when he writes that the movies, in less than a quarter of a century, *will go by another name* and will become *the magical art of alchemists, which it never should have stopped being: entrancing, capable of bringing the spectators, in each fraction of a second, this unknown feeling of ubiquity in a fourth dimension, suppressing space and time...*

When the crisis erupts in the United States in the thirties, the American producers and directors discover that the very technique of film itself can save them from the slump and invest them with an important social and economic mission: the deferred time of the cinematographic motor empties the present world of appearances, the ubiquity allows millions of spectators that haunt the auditoriums (consigned to film like trains are to travel) to forget their material plight.

Sandrich, who will contribute to the fame of the dancer Fred Astaire, demands geometrical decors, where white and black, shadow and light, seem violently contrasted, effacing the impression of relief and volume. The dancer himself, dressed in black and white, will evolve in continuity before a fixed-position camera, or nearly. Fred Astaire's smoking jacket, with hemmed stitches of thin shiny bands, his dances that are mostly only stylizations of walking or of the most ordinary gestures of life, all of this is, finally, only a variation on the themes of Marey's chronophotography.[4] Certain spectators couldn't stand this kind of treatment for long and found themselves plunged into a restorative sleep after only a few minutes of projection.

However, one of the official photographers of Fred Astaire was the famous Edward Steichen, former director of aerial operations of the American expeditionary force in France during the First World War.

From 1914, due to war photographs taken from little recon-
naissance planes, there was progress in the chronophotographic
technique. The belligerents applied industrial methods of
work-division and intensive production of images to aerial
surveillance: in 1916 the French established a military film
library: and Colonel Steichen, for his part, will gather almost
1,300,000 pictures which, after the war, will wind up in his
personal collection. And a good number of these photographs
will be exhibited and sold under the name of their author and
as his property. Later, symptomatically, the photography galleries
of the Museum of Modern Art will be dedicated to Steichen.

But what interests us in the taking of these millions of
pictures "for the purpose of the systematic exploration of
traces of the enemy in the landscape, so as to destroy same" is
the new prosthetic synergy in process. This new harmony
that blends motor, eye and weapon. This alchemy of meaning, capable this time, in a single anamorphosis, of revealing
an instability that precipitates every form toward its ruin, this
instrumental collage that allows, minute by minute, day-
after-day, the erosion of a building, a trench, a city or a
countryside, under the combined effect of long-distance
bombardments and the ubiquitous gaze of military leaders.
As Allan Sekula writes, in a remarkable text devoted to Steichen, "the meaning of the aerial photo, its *reading*, depends
on all that can be drawn from the rationalized act of inter-
pretation as a source of military intelligence... few pictures,
except possibly in the medical field, are as 'free,' seemingly,
from a meaning higher than that of their usage..."

And so the idea imposes itself progressively that this synergy of eye and motor, realized in the camera, was not, after all, restricted to this apparatus; the visual prosthesis could from now on melt into the production systems, together with those designed to transport bodies. Moholy-Nagy and various members of the Bauhaus, benefiting from their war experiences, "aerialize" their pictures by climbing over the roofs and fire escapes of tall buildings (about 1920). For his part, Abel Gance declares that you have to shoulder your camera, ride on horseback, bicycle, sled, swing.

Double exposure was a technique of the silent movies that saw itself somewhat as the translation into images of the theatrical aside. Destined to reveal their thoughts and feelings, it makes the face of the stars seen in fixed close-up even more inhuman, literally pierced by battle-landscapes, sea, sky, roads, unchained elements... but finally this process reproduces the visual sensation you feel at day's end, when, during a trip, you look at your own reflection or that of another in the train or automobile window, traversed by the tumult of a landscape fleeing like an arrow.[5] Double exposure will significantly be replaced by the "traveling shot," realized from a moving automobile.

From now on when he shouts "motor" to his assistants, the driver-moviemaker is not so much after making the background-decor parade before him as to cross it, even to pierce through it to the light beyond. Like the war weapon launched at full speed at the visual target it's supposed to wipe out, the aim of cinema will be to provoke an effect of vertigo in the voyeur-traveler, the end being sought now is to give him the impression of being projected into the image. The star will no longer be the luminous specter of the landscape, the leading lady of the scene from now on will be the mass of spectators. Jim Collins remarks, for example, that in Fred Astaire's *Swingtime* "the first level is a subjective level from the point-of-view of an imaginary spectator placed on a balcony while the rest of the audience remains perfectly visible on the screen, a little beneath, and Astaire on the stage." This reproduces the projection conditions of the old traveling moviehouses, such as described by Gaston Bonheur: "The *screen* was a sheet hung in the mayor's barn. We students sat in the *first row*, awaiting impatiently the twilight cowboy hour when our young leaping shadows mixed with the lusty stampedes unleashed by buffalo and mustangs."

Before being transformed, significantly, into parking lots, the moviehouse had been enlarged considerably, into a veritable dark temple whose roof was conjured away and where false constellations glimmer in the absorbent planetarium blue. Along with the sound of electric organs and the whir of projectors, clever gradations of half-day and of blacklight was part of the show, conditioning the spectators that found themselves fluorescent in their turn, emitting a mysterious light. Everything happened in the multitude of luminous signals of a common transport that suddenly would become the common transmutation of species, moment of inertia when everything is already there, in the *false day* of the speed of liberation of light—which effectively frees us from the voyage—in favor of the attentive impatience for a world that does not stop coming, that we can't stop waiting for.

We loved then those cartoons showing gracious little mythical characters, tearing themselves like cuttings from the paper sheet of the draftsman who created them, to haunt his apartment and perturb his worktable, messing around in their turn with his pens and pencils. These types of tricks, introducing the cartoons into photographed decors, also accomplished that metamorphosis in the look of the real that the spectator was anticipating. A new hierarchy of dimensions, the intense visualization succeeded touch, contact with matter; everyday visionary, plaything of a collective hallucination, each spectator passed effortlessly from the rectangle of the sheet of paper or easel painting to that of the screen and onto the synoptic machination of surface effects.

This congruence of eye and motor controlled everything from then on, right up to the very découpage of the script; a new truth of vision metamorphosed the rhythms of life itself. No need any longer for preliminary exposition of facts and places, so important in theatrical work: before the film begins, the spectator already has an idea of what awaits him, the simpler the script the more likely he is to find the spectacle amusing. Finally he needs only to follow the traces of the slolum, to follow with his gaze the sequences of the parade, where all logic, all reaction become accidental. Suspense, the kind of halt where the action stops so as to develop in the spectator the artificial anguish as to what is going to happen, reappears finally in the scenario of the accelerated voyage:

"When I go for a walk in the forest," writes a contemporary, "I'm evidently exposed to the fall of a tree, to the attack of a marauder, but these are very rare risks. If, on the contrary, I find myself in a car going 60 mph on the Fontainebleu road on Sunday, my situation has become much more chancey... The fate of the driver has become pure chance."

Speed treats vision like its basic element; with acceleration, to travel is like filming, not so much producing images as new mnemonic traces, unlikely, supernatural. In such a context death itself can no longer be felt as mortal; it becomes, as in William Burroughs, a simple technical accident, the final separation of the sound from the picture track. Whether the Titanic or Zeppelin the fatal catastrophe seems to passengers of the giant vehicle like a senseless, unreal hypothesis, and while the ship sinks they continue to dance to the sound of the orchestra. But the disparity between the holiday illusion and the occurrence of the accidental is only apparent, since accelerated flight or rapid travel have insidiously metamorphosed the festival by making of disaster the destiny and pleasure of the trip. Is it not, therefore, the desire for this holiday experienced essentially as *without tomorrow* that has pushed generations towards the cosmopolitanism of trains and transatlantic travel, toward the international palaces and temples of film, even before they were sold self-service travel in the supermarkets?

"To see the landscape pass by a train or automobile window or to look at a film or computer screen the way you look out of a window, unless even the train or the cockpit become in their turn projection rooms... train, car, jet, telephone, television... our whole life passes by in the prostheses of accelerated voyages, of which we are no longer even conscious... '*the need for peregrination has led to the establishment in displacement itself of the very fixity of life.*'[6]

Where are we when we travel? In the supplementary day that Phineas Fogg, circular traveler of Jules Verne's novel, had counted as added onto the 80 days of circumnavigation, and which, for his London friends had never existed? It's quite evident that Phineas' accelerated trip had led only to that, the ensemble of borrowed vehicles had made for him a false day. But the brave Wulff "satellized" by the malicious Fandor "waiting for the end of the line on a circular roadway,"[7] doesn't he also find a megalopolis that no longer existed: "I visited Paris," he exclaims when they dragged him finally from his railway car, "it's a huge city, I've counted 127 stations since this morning, been on the train for five hours and we've crossed ten rivers..."

The popularity of music halls waned during the times of economic depression between the wars. The film temples, palaces, transatlantic boats, were, so to speak, emptied from one day to the next, and now it's the turn of television, in the developed countries, to lose millions of spectators every year. They speak each time of temporary crisis, but in fact when a technique dies it's replaced by another that's considered more effective, for none of the changes are independent, all comprise a single basic quest for the prostheses of subliminal comfort.

About film, for example, they've discussed for a long time the matter of hypnagogic habits; they've compared the spectator to the child celebrating, in darkness, his falling-asleep rite. We've analyzed right up to the very ice cream sandwiches ("Eskimo Tits") sold during intermission, melting merchandise that will be slowly sucked during the projection and will favor installation in different states of worldly perception.

In London, after the last World War, and while the populations were still subjected to drastic alimentary and economic restrictions, the moviehouses stayed open practically 24 hours a day.

So some people spent the quasi-totality of their existence there, for a modest price. The cinema could create at will the occasion, an entry into another logic; there you could escape the effects of peace, just as you had previously escaped those of war by taking up residence in a subway corridor. Furthermore, the true amateur goes to the movies alone and can't tolerate any noise in his vicinity or any movement foreign to the spectacle. The price of the seat becomes a sort of real estate value adjusted to the ensemble of the circumstances: the most expensive are the large and deep kind of the Pullman type, while the movable hard benches are cheaper. Alfred Hitchcock's motto, "The movies are, first of all, armchairs with spectators inside," means something entirely different than commercialism. The spectator's armchair is like Jean Renoir's at his life's end: "Give my wheelchair a push," he says to his secretary. "I'm like a slow moving camera."

The film industry will enter into crisis when it ends production of the false day, when it pretends to verisimilitude.

Realism of the script, vulgarization of the actors, precision of color photography, CinemaScope or Cinerama, everything is arranged to awake attention, right up to the traveling shot, speeding up and pretending to communicate to the voyeur-voyager a kind of vehicular drunkenness worthy of the scenic railway, an identification of the passenger with the meteoric velocity of the course. Conscious of the new complicity between industrial film (films whose makers are production groups rather than individuals) and the automobile industry, the "society-of-the spectacle" people, however, are mistaken about the causes of the success attained by individual transportation machines: the mass automobile is not a model made for dandies-of-the-motor rocketing in search of vertiginous sensations, and the success of the plush little sports cars and showy American luxury models after the war ought to have alerted the manufacturers.

The huge lines of spectators jostling each other Saturday and Sunday before the windows of the temples of film are disappearing because they reform from now on, and as punctually, at the freeway entrances. It's simply the case that what had pushed the masses toward the cinema armchairs now forces them into the seats of their automobiles.

From this perspective, the evolution of moviehouses may be revealed as useful for analysis of the cities: the immense and obscure nave yields to little compartmentalized volumes that recall strangely the character of cells of means of transportation. Minimum transit space, maximum of armchair on the smallest possible surface, the era of the great monuments of the spectacle seems to be over, the new Opéra is the Boeing 747, a projection room where they try to compensate for the monotony of the trip by the attraction of the image, festival of aerial crossings, transitory dis-urbanization where nomadic micropoles replace the sedentary metropoles, and where the world–flown-over offers nothing further of interest, to the point where the Supersonic's subliminal comfort demands the world's total occlusion, in anticipation probably of the next phase—flight-in-darkness and narcosis of the passengers. The question today therefore is no longer to know if cinema can do without a place but if places can do without cinema. Urbanism is in decline, architecture is in constant movement, while dwellings have become no more than anamorphoses of thresholds. In spite of people nostalgic about History, Rome is no longer in Rome, architecture no longer in architecture, but in geometry; the space-time of vectors, the aesthetic of construction is dissimulated in the special effects of the communication machines, engines of transfer and transmission; the arts continue to disappear in the intense illumination of projection and diffusion. After the age of architecture-sculpture we are now in the time of cinematographic factitiousness; literally as well as figuratively, from now on *architecture is only a movie*; an un-habitual motility is successor to the habitudes of the city, become an immense darkroom for the fascination of the mobs, where the light of vehicular speed (audiovisual and automobile) renews the glare of solar light; the city is no longer a theatre (agora, forum) but the cinema of city lights: they've returned to *Ur* (*Our*, light), believing now that the desert is without horizon.

In his car the voyeur-voyager rediscovers the comportment of the votary of the giant screen, or even that of the cosmopolitan fauna of the beginning of the century: "Men and women who share a voyage are no longer themselves... every passenger begins his trip by leaving himself behind; yesterday they didn't know each other, tomorrow they'll be forever separated..."[8] The speed of the transport only multiplies the absence; travel to forget, they used to advise the neurasthenic, traveling lessens the suicidal tension in opposing a substitute for it; the little death of the departure, the gain acquired in the increase in rapidity of displacement was a disappearance into a holiday where there's no tomorrow, which amounts, for each, to a deferred rehearsal of his *last day*.

The extreme realism of recent cinematographic productions was no longer capable of satisfying the expectations of voyeur-voyagers, "dialectical unity of the real and the unreal," Marcel L'Herbier called it, but also instantaneous mixing of the voyage where rapports of proximity weaken, the gap increasing or lessening as the case may be, the bizarre becomes banal and the common spectacle, the world without memory.

Better yet, the locomotive illusion allows the voyeur-voyager to project beyond the screen of the windshield his own fantasies. The UFOs, those luminous objects that witnesses do not succeed in classifying in their memories of the real world and that, nevertheless, many people claim to have seen, demonstrate to what extent technical effects have become capable of afflicting us with paramnesia.

In the American film, *Close Encounters of the Third Kind*, the apparition of UFOs is assimilated to the production on the screen of luminous emissions, reconnecting with the spirit and the works of Marey. This production was very successful commercially and created a new model for emulation.

Today the great number of these kinds of films, which combine visual and sonic electronic effects, is causing problems for television, technically incapable of creating these new gnoses in the spectators. When the fascist Marinetti and his followers, avid for motion-power, thought up the anthropocentric superman (coming identification of man and motor), they envisioned the metal claws, the disappearance of bodies in the cumbersome prostheses that technology then produced.

A little in the style of Edgar Poe, in the story where a wounded veteran becomes a patchwork of organs and grafted members, a sort of mechanical doll able to take itself apart and to disappear completely when it wants to rest. But they didn't realize that to identify with the motor was to identify with the vector, as Burroughs remarks about language: "It is a component of the body like any other... Words are micro-organisms, living dust that the electronic revolution only assembles and orders, right up to the differentiated levels of meaning."

We haven't pondered enough on the basic causes of the generalized evolution of technology: *miniaturization*, reducing to nothing or next-to-nothing the size of every machine, is not only to furnish replacement parts to the organism by placing them on the scale of the human body, it is also to create inside the person a parasensory competition, a duplication of being in the world.

If in 1978 American television lost five to six million watchers who stopped turning on their screens at a certain hour, the old automobile industry meanwhile had no trouble overcoming the effects of the energy crisis that certain experts had forecast was to be fatal. The frantic use of automobiles or motorcycles is not, contrary to public transportation, for the purpose of going somewhere in particular; here it is not *a priori* a question of distances to cross, which creates inevitably new travel conditions. To go nowhere, even to ride around in a deserted quarter or on a crowded freeway, now seems natural for the voyeur-voyager in his car. On the contrary, to stop, to park, are unpleasant operations and the driver even resents going somewhere or toward someone; to visit a person or to go see a show seems to require superhuman effort.

Able to reach the farthest extremities, he's not happy except in the narrow cell of his vehicle, strapped into his seat. Like the moviegoer he knows in advance what he's going to see, the script; the lack of variation of landscapes scoured by speed favors the driver's attempts to identify with the vector. If most drivers are still not yet capable of utilizing a complex electronic language, of combining the transportation of bodies and of information, at least the headlights and parking lights seem already a means of primary emission, a sort of formulation of desire and of a new presence that drivers are happy to abuse. They mimic the increasingly powerful lights on official vehicles and enjoy blinding with their light-signals the passengers of other cars. Likewise drivers that are alone keep the radio on constantly, to hear voices and not to listen to any particular show. In the discos, which reproduce very closely the old movie palace effects, dancers like to be alone on the floor… alone in the middle of the crowd, protected by the amplifying action of 7,000 watts and by laser rays. The same thing will be observed by social workers about aged and isolated people: "They complain about being abandoned and yet they find it repugnant to *see* or to be seen by people, to be in direct physical contact with people: they prefer using the telephone to tell their secrets into what they call their *artificial ears.*" Having left the movie palace behind the voyeur-voyagers have escaped the factitiousness of that world only to accomplish its realization, as Ray Bradbury suggests, carrying out "the wills of Rembrandt and Walt Disney."

A former Disney co-worker recounts: "Walt's imagination worked like a motor at full-throttle… you know how he got the idea of Disneyland? One day he put his daughters on a merry-go-round. While it was spinning he was waiting on a bench munching peanuts. He was thinking that there ought to be *a place where parents and children could enjoy themselves together*… In short, after the ride the idea was born, and then realized in 1955, in a terrain of about 20 square miles in Los

Angeles: Disneyland, the first amusement park conceived in *trompe-l'oeil*."[9]

Here again the return to principle becomes the condition of success, return to the ancient device of the wooden horses with the horsemen playing at catching the rings on their toy spears; stupefying fake absences, where each becomes the passenger of a giant phenakistoscope, that other ancestor of the comic strip. Then comes Disneyland, where Méliès' disciple will extend his power even farther over the world's appearances, organizing a city the way his predecessor faked his films: "The impact of Disneyland and Disney World," says another collaborator, comes from Walt's *cinematic know-how*: ideas, instead of entering in competition, complete and prolong each other. If the pedestrian is so comfortable in our kingdoms, it's because the size of the buildings and means of transportation is reduced a fifth of their normal dimension. Nothing, neither trains, nor the identically duplicated cars, is on a normal scale, which creates… the dream." Here the stroller is like Jean Renoir in his wheelchair, functioning like a camera, while the anamorphosis is created by an alteration of dimensions, a falsification of the factors of distance and appearance.

The nihilism of technique destroys the world less surely than the nihilism of speed destroys the world's truth, as Paul de Kock wrote in 1842: "The railroad is nature's true magic lantern." Which the clock-worshipper Charles V also expressed in his way, in his definition of Empire as where "the sun never sets." For the conquering emperor, whose attack on the world never relents, *a single day is like a thousand years* and the conquered earth is reduced to the light of this single day—finally, the object of this conquest, that is of the king-of-the-road's desire, is assimilated to the speed of light.[10]

Likewise, the victor will say to the vanquished on the night after the battle: "This day was not yours!"

A witness reports that the court of the Spanish Bourbons "functioned like those German cuckoo clocks where the same characters appear and disappear every day at the same time." Just as the battlefield accorded the day to the polemarch, so the monarch derives from the protocol of identical days the sensation of living a single eternal day. The concrete result of the quest for absolute power was, in the times of the early Valois, the periodical creation of great assemblies where all were invited—festivals, sports events, the invention of what they called "incomparable days"… likewise, the carnival, that originally lasted from the Day of Kings to Ash Wednesday, was extended by the Venetians to the duration of six months.

Beyond all these Jupiter or Apollo myths, the production of light is associated with power, since light, as speed, is also only a vector. You can follow the decadence of the French monarchy by walking through the paths of the park of Versailles, from the Palace to the Trianon and finally to the Queen's Hamlet. You might ask yourself what motivates such a deployment of art, but these arts are, above all, artifacts in the most literal sense, artificial structures or phenomena encountering and dealing with natural phenomena, all feeling reduced here to an optical illusion. With the development of fireworks we know also of the importance of water effects in this kind of palace, representation at the same time of the mechanical vector and of the diversity of its intensities... a sun in each drop of water, the spectacle of water-in-movement renders palpable the illusion that hits us. This "nature that places the mask of the visible on the invisible" and that, according to Hugo, "is *only an appearance corrected by a transparency.*" At Vaux-le-Vicomte, the projection of water into space is effectuated by successive sequences that are superimposed until finally the image of the chateau in the eye of the spectator is *drowned*, totally clouded; a *perpetuum mobile* mechanism consisting precisely in harmonizing optimally the passage of one form into another, up to the now instantaneous threshold of their disappearance. As the absolute power of the monarch declines the cinematics of water also disappear: at the Queen's Hamlet they create false pools where water stagnates as in the Lilliputian *arsenalos* of the Spanish Bourbons that contemporaries called pissholes. The last monarch lived alongside their palaces, in "maidservant's quarters," attempting an everyday realism quite contrary to the inimitable day with no tomorrow of triumphant royalty. They create agendas that will have no more than a very distant connection with their rigidities of protocol and the realities of whatever lonely power they still retain.

In turn clockmakers, shoemakers, locksmiths, will all soon be accused of insanity when we see them attempt, like Louis II of Bavaria, to repopulate palaces and recreate the illusory day of the court.

We're here at the heart of the iconoclastic quarrel, of the coupling of bodies with objects of unusual brilliance.

As with the famous "iron crown" offered by Theodeline to her husband the Duke of Turin in 594 and which was made of a ring of iron covered with blades of gold. Contemporaries affirmed that it was made this way for the purpose of showing those who wore it that power is a burden which is dissimulated under a false glitter. The aura, the refulgence precedes the loss of consciousness and attacks the spectator's will, light of the great void or nimbus encircling the visage of the deified emperor, and also that of Christ and the Saints, helmets studded with gems, tiaras, diadems, the insignia of power are also efficacious prostheses of a royal nirvana that transforms the assistance of the state into manipulation of subjects by the Prince. Disgrace, political misfortune, is the exile that distances from this central light and descends into darkness, or even into prison, which is not so much lock-up as burial, privation of the light of day in subterranean jails, windowless cells.

Agnes Varda said of the making of her film, *Happiness*: "I thought about the impressionists because in their canvases is *a luminosity which corresponds to a certain definition of happiness... If there is drama, it is provoked by the desire for happiness pushed to the extreme limit.*" We can abbreviate Varda's formula simply by replacing the word happiness with the definition she gives of it and we obtain an even more explicit sentence: "If there's a drama it is provoked by the desire for luminosity pushed to its extreme limit."[11]

To produce prostheses of subliminal comfort is to produce *simulators of day*, even of the last day, metamorphosis of the objects of industrial production where the ensemble of economic realities would be the relay for the cinematic function.

The Disney firm spent $17.5 million producing a new science fiction film: *The Black Hole* (Harrison Ellenshaw's special effects, which accounted for only 13 matte shots in *Star Wars*, are involved—through the unprecedented use of a camera maneuvered by computer in 110 of them in this film).

But at the same time, associated with numerous governments, encouraged by NATO, aided by industrial enterprises and their scientists, the firm is in the process of creating EPCOT (Experimental Prototype Community of Tomorrow), which will not be "a factory for ideas, but an idea in action," capable, as Disney wished it to be, "of making you forget present troubles and death... the real world."

Assuming responsibility for desire by the various powers is by now no longer the adoption of responsibility by various vectors, but that of expectations, of all expectations made possible by the outfitting of the body. So this "political spectacle" that the French recently have found so entertaining is already obsolete in the United States, where the voters are increasingly rare, in the sense that the only true majority is a *motorized* one, acquiring "good reflexes" along with the driving license, that is, the habit of reacting to conditioning stimuli—and where the latest way of getting their attention is to multiply light and sound signals and no longer the images of hypothetical actor candidates. Inversely, technical failure will from now on be able to supplant error in political or economic projection: France had a chance to confirm this, after America, on "Black Tuesday," when, on December 19, 1978 at 8:27 the relay of electrical current was suddenly stopped at the German border: this "general rehearsal for *an even darker future...*" threatened the directors of Electricity of France. On a very cold day, at a time when traffic was extremely heavy—a week before Christmas—the time was ripe for plunging the urban populations into *the greatest anguish*. This time the drama also grew from the incontinence of the desire for luminosity and for manipulation of the night.

A year earlier, in October 1977 in Houston, the laboratory that for several years had been using the telemetric instruments left on the moon by "Apollo" ceased functioning; the control screens suddenly went off, and since then nothing has moved on the dead star. Soon the only thing left will be for us to forget the specious distinction between the propagation of images or waves and that of objects or bodies, since from now on all duration will be measured in intensity.

3

To the extent that its principle theme comes down to: *science technology of other worlds*, the revival of science fiction in the United States and in the industrialized nations seems linked to that of religions and sects. If on the one hand people like Professor Lawrence Leshan are pointing out the similarity in vision of the universe and its laws in atomic physicists and in the great mystics,[1] the science fiction narrative, on the other hand, demonstrates the incompatibilities existing between our presence in the world and the various levels of a certain anesthesia in our consciousness that, at every moment, inclines us to see-saw into more or less extensive absences, more or less serious, even to provoke by various means instantaneous immersions in other worlds, parallel worlds, interstitial, bifurcating, right up to that *black hole*, which would be only an excess of speed in these kinds of crossings, a pure phenomenon of speed, abrogating the initial separation between day and night.

Responding to a new anxious question, this type of narrative only adapts, faithfully enough, the Judeo-Christian version of Genesis *in having science and especially the technical media play the logistical role initially acted by the first woman.* Satan,[2] appearing in the Bible as seducer of woman who in turn seduces man, commences then the cycle of humanity sworn less to death than to disappearance, that is to expulsion from the world in which it has lived, this being accomplished, initially, as a phenomenon of consciousness. In effect, the physical expulsion from the Earthly Paradise is preceded by a brutal disruption of vision that completely changed the appearance of the world inhabited by the couple: their eyes are opened, they see they're naked, they cover their nudity, they seek to veil themselves, to hide from God. What is involved here is a stunning succession of visual phenomena, and not, as we like to think, a sexual innovation. In fact, seduction, the leading astray of *seducere*, assumes here a cosmo-dynamic dimension, seduction is a rite-of-passage from one world to another that implies a major departure for humanity, the beginning of a navigation of body and sense from something immovable toward another category of Time, a space-time essentially different because it is sensed as instable, mobile, conductive, transformable, like the creation of a second universe depending entirely on this initial rite-of-passage.

The leading astray of seduction is therefore inscribed precisely in the dynamics of this world; there woman is not possessive, possessed or possessing, but attractive; the force of attraction is in fact gravitation, universal weight, *axis mundi*.

Mistress of the passage, she has until now effectively organized all that speed is, all that takes part in the movement of man's life is inscribed in her, and all that competes with it.

This beloved, who, according to Novalis, is *the microcosm* of a universe which is only *an extension* of the loved one, the body of the woman becoming one with a communication body, is the ideal vector between man and the new world— it's no longer simply a matter of a couple, but of a sort of triangle. The solitary movement of *seducere* or sexual coupling necessitating solidarity in movement—the couple is also a yoking, a coupling, the constitution of an effect of common discipline, a kind of two-seater vehicle, implying the territorial body as a third partner.[3]

In the episode of Genesis we observe that the rites-of-passage from one world to the other provoke not only a metamorphosis of vision but also an immediate dissimulation, a prudent camouflage of bodies. We may recall here the reflection of Hannah Arendt: terror is the end of the law of movement.

In the Biblical story fear is contemporaneous with seduction because the latter is precisely production of the exceptional phenomenon of speed, so that the anticipation of an accident occurs instantly.

The "sin" of the first man: isn't it called familiarly the "fall," the ancients thus establishing a direct relation between what they've agreed to call original sin and this earthly weight that they considered to be a natural motor of the free acceleration of bodies, of their projection, but also of their collision?

When Alain Schlokoff (producer of "Science Fiction Film Week") elaborates on the replacement of erotic and porno films by horror films, saying that *sex no longer exists* and that *fear has replaced it*, we should not underestimate the importance of this modification of mass sensibility. In fact the solitary pleasure derived by the spectator of porno films through the cinematographic motor announces already the foreshortening which is beginning and which is comparable to that of the science fiction story in relation to the Biblical hypothesis: that is the disappearance of human intermediaries and the emergence of a sexuality directly connected to the technical object, provided that the latter is a motor, a vector of movement; the horror film then succeeds the erotic film as a more perfect fulfillment of the law of movement in a universe where technological progress corresponds to the utilization and the search for extreme speeds. We may also notice in the evolution of the technical vehicle a succession of representations of sexual coupling. The resemblance between the seat and the back-support position of the arm passed around the figure or the thighs, the invention of the moving seat (carry chair) and that of the first automobiles (Ford, Daimler, Benz) of the rolling wheelchair variety. The similarity between the interior of the car and that of the alcove, the double bed and right up to the vibrating beds used in brothels that also evoke the common voyage of coupling.

If terror is the accomplishment of the law of movement, attraction itself can convey anguish. Attracting the gaze is to capture it and thereby to subvert attention, the optical illusion in a world entirely perceived as illusion. The trans-sexual game renews the horizon's power of attraction, the invitation to the voyage. Jean Gabin, seduced by the actress Michèle Morgan, accosts her with these words: "With those eyes you must travel a lot and take quite a few along with you!" Today, if a girl wants, strictly speaking, to "follow a guy," it amounts for her to thumbing a ride, taking pleasure with another by "leaving regular hours behind." But in the practice of hitch-hiking the crisis of dimensions intervenes directly, it's the vector automobile that becomes the condensation of the universe, the loved one is no longer "extended," she is reduced, restrained to the immediacy of ubiquity until terror, crime or rape comes to fulfill the law of movement. The speed of displacement has perverted the Kidnapping of the Beauty, the ancient nuptial rape, into a means of disappearance and extermination.

At one time, in the institutions, the education of little-girls-in-uniform, strict discipline, was aimed at making of the child a creator of artifacts, as a constant reference to the marvelous mechanicalness of the body vector of the woman, but also to her supposed absence of intelligence and original ideas.[4] Deportment, ornament, manners, dance, were useful for the camouflage of *physical identity*, of nature and its failures.

Ignorance, even sexual indifference, gave these "silly geese" greater dependability, for the execution of a continually repeated series of maneuvers destined to subjugate those around them and especially the chosen partner is the only effective protection against a male society that condemned dowered girls to an early marriage, others to menial labor, the convent, to prostitution or to destitution. We should keep in mind, however, that Jean-Jacques de Cambaceres, who participated in the creation of a new legal code, so precious to 19th and 20th century bourgeois husbands, was homosexual—which seems almost logical in a militarizing society, revalorizing the ornament of the warrior couple, the coupling of the homosexual duel, living at the rhythm of the distance-of-conquest. For the Duke of Parma, the heterosexuality of the Napoleonic couple takes on the quality of an obligatory but sinister formality, a conjugal duty, assuring the procreation necessary for the survival of the new Military State, a remedy for decimation, and no longer legitimation for some kind of desire of the other sex. As to our Latin Napoleon— he's caught the cult of the mother, of the reign of the terrorizing Jocasta who's invented discrimination, the superiority of the son over the female offspring.

The scorn of heterosexuality and the dissimulation of corporeity express, in the end, only a repulsion of the superman-warrior for a logistically devalued partner. From now on, the less a woman looks like one the greater her chances of pleasing, since, as the slogan says, "fighters are always of the same sex."

From George Sand to Marlene Dietrich, both coming from military societies and families, the homosexual artifice will be expertly used as a means of seduction and also of social liberation. Marshal de Saxe's descendant, by adopting a male first name, masculine clothes and manias, enhances herself.

With her partners she never lets go completely, declaring that, in the end, no man had been able to give her as much pleasure as she could give herself.

According to George Sand, the woman artist is first of all a voyager, a wanderer; her model is the chaste Consuelo disguising herself as a boy and abolishing the difference between the sexes through her scorn for "mortal loves"…

Likewise the *romantic* novel can easily stop at the marriage, not through prudery, but because the young woman's technical exploit is then completed; she has led the husband astray, the rites-of-passage of hymen are no longer her business, and she'll often find in the conjugal bed her reasons for a cold and definitive hatred of her awkward husband. Actually comparable to the performance of the transvestite (they used to speak more precisely before of transvesticism which also suggests the travelo or drag queen), the moving performance of the "silly goose" already announces the claim of *women in movement* of the Women's Movement: *we are not sexual objects*.

To Aragon's slogan: *woman is man's future*, the Women's Movement replied: man is the past of woman, each seeking finally to increase the division by installing the partner in a *deferred time* of the great navigation of the species.

One finds, furthermore, in the styles of love, a pendulum effect signifying this kind of distention: suffragettes and other woman's emancipation groups are particularly active after wars, the great deadly conflicts of males. On the other hand, the sentimental, romantic periods are more likely before or during revolutions and conflicts. The fact is that the military mobilization is above all an invitation to travel and also substitutes there for "amorous transport." The young woman "who gives herself to the *mobilized* soldier before he's left and because he might not be coming back" is a well-known type. As if the loved one wanted one last time to participate in the energy of the journey. But what is aimed at here again is the relegation of the partner as well as the world of war that will instantly place the man in the past of the woman. Inversely, the hastily concluded "war marriage," as we call it, would be for the most part ephemeral; when the soldier has the lame idea of returning safe and sound to the woman's present life he's rejected.

Little by little the tragic character of the necessity of seduction, of ceaselessly seducing is revealed; it's like an exorbitant inflation of the law of movement and of the vectorial faculties of bodies, an acceleration of the irresistible disappearance of the partners in space and time; to lead them astray is to lead them to nothingness and it is in this sense that seductive activity interferes with technical fatality and more precisely with the technique of war, as described by Colonel Delair: an art that must be ceaselessly transformed and does not escape the general law of the world: to stay in the same place is to die.

The famous *Song of Leaving* also shows this give-and-take between techniques of war and love:

"Go, valiant husbands, battles are your holidays…" exclaims the choir, before reassuring the future heroes: "And if the temple of memory opened to your conquering manes, our voices will sing your glory, our flanks will bear your avengers..."

"Many women have loved themselves in me," confessed Franz Liszt. We discover in this phrase the notion of the multiplication of speed and conquest and at the same time that of reciprocal invisibility. Not only is the partner "one of those relay horses you mount once, then see no more," as they used to say under the Ancien Regime, but the rapprochement of *making love*, that immediate commutation of persons, doesn't abolish the inaccessibility previously created by the separations of distance and difference.

Besides, nothing is easier than to eliminate your partner without, for that matter, leaving him or her for even a second. As with old couples, each of the parties has become invisible to the other through repetition of a limited number of signs, smells, movements and common manias accomplished daily, so that they are already known and expected by the partner—what they call, abusing the term, intimacy. As real time slides by and age increases, the attenuation of perception creates a new cinematic anamorphosis, since aged people change to such an extent their "temporal point of view" that they're quite able to speak in detail of an event that took place 40 years ago as if it happened yesterday, meanwhile totally forgetting what has happened recently. The pretention to everyday realism is here only a kind of *résumé of the plot*, a little like those disaster film sequences acted out by stuntmen that we've understood could not have been projected in real time, the suddenness of the accident implying such a quantity of events developing in an amount of time so brief that the natural eye, incapable of seizing it all, is content to summarize it. The narrative time seems incompatible with vision, and in order to try to see, it will become paradoxically necessary to introduce a disordering of vision—*slow motion*.

The old man adopts an attitude close to the child that he was; abrogating his adult age, he desires like a little boy asked about what he wants for Christmas, "*everything to be the way it was*, exiles to come home, those that were killed or who died to be alive again..." For him the crucial point is the place of things, what's there and suddenly is not, what's disappeared for always seems to him unbearable. As in the tale told endlessly to children the phrase *once upon a time* at the beginning of the story is irreplaceable. Furthermore, the storyteller must make sure that nothing changes and not to add flourishes or omit anything. One who commits these errors is liable to immediate recriminations from the young listeners. The fairy tale is marvelous not only for the extraordinary adventures it narrates but also because these always stay the same, forever identical to the point of seeming unique. This kind of anesthesia, provoked by the repetition of attitudes-rendered-banal, is utilized also by secret services that have created a very particular category of spies, that of *sleepers*. The sleeper is, first of all, a social phantasm. He must live in an enemy milieu, work, have a career, marry, have children—like a pawn that serves no purpose in the game of international espionage and who possibly will never serve any… unless one day he is ordered to *activate*. He then projects into his mission the material proofs of his long illusory existence. It is the high degree of his banality that lends him the invisibility necessary to accomplish, without arousing the suspicions of his neighbors, the particular task he's suddenly been ordered to perform. Sir Anthony Blunt, famous British personality and artistic advisor to the Queen, former Cambridge professor, was only unmasked twenty years after his old students and accomplices. Guy Burgess and Donald MacLean, two diplomats who had one day mysteriously disappeared, reappearing in Moscow in 1951. But they were all working for the Russians from well before World War II.

The vehicular attraction of the coupling, before being renewed by the technical object, had engendered zoophilism as another form of heterosexuality.[5] The horse in particular was treated like a god by the polemarch, even solemnly married. Reserve of power, source of speed in combat, but beyond that the zoophilous cult likes proposing the image of the hybrid animal. The bulls are winged or sphinxes have lions' bodies and human heads; later they are represented as winged and feminized.

At Thebes the Sphinx is the keeper of a hidden wisdom, she interpolates and proposes annoying riddles to those on the road, passers-by and travelers; wrong answers cause the brutal annihilation, the decimation of the unfortunate. The enigma proposed by the Sphinx to Oedipus is a question on the *strange being that moves through time*, and it is really the diversity of techniques used by the being that is the basis for the interrogation; it is this very diversity that in turn designates man among other animals.

The (metabolic) vehicle is here rendered as the *enigma of movement* and wrong answers to this enigma come under the sanctions of the predatory animal, the blend of zoophilism from the powerful body recoups murderous energies under a peaceful exterior, supple and often caressing, like that of the great felines (cat family) whose hair trigger responses are unpredictable.

Zoophilism and its hybrids prefigures technophilism and its amalgamations. Ford's social project for the American economy announced already the synergy being formed between techniques of production, the manufactured product and corporeity itself—the figure of the consumer-worker united in and through indivisible speed. But in Liszt's formula, the movement of romantic passions, through the oversupply of energy and acceleration of amorous transport, what is meant is rather a rivalry than an opposition—or an alliance between the metabolic and the technical, an absolute valorization of rites-of passage and their number, to the detriment of bodies themselves and their presence in the world.

Succeeding or opposing the deadly male (warrior), the *femme fatale* is rarely a beautiful woman, she's worse. Stendhal observes about Angela Pietragrua, who he's in love with: "I don't know what made her tell me that friends had said she frightened them. It's true... You'd think she was some kind of superior being that had assumed beauty because that disguise suited her better than another, and who, with her penetrating eyes, could read into your soul…"

One is struck by the physical austerity of famous courtisanes, by the contrast the body offers to the magnificence of their finery, the animated brilliance of the weapons of seduction. Here also, physiological identity disappears behind the allure of a technical valorization, so that many of these women will continue to exert their functions until an advanced age, 70 or 80 for some who are still being recompensed. Nor is it rare to see one of them attain to the summit of the state hierarchy, or inversely, for women of high social standing to measure themselves by the standards of prostitutes and yield themselves up to veritable marathons, speed records in receiving passengers of the sexual voyage, high productivity which causes them to be considered men's equals—monarchs, or rather polemarchs. Once more, acceleration of the transient rite implied an eco-sexuality, the presence of a territorial immensity and the *seducere* could no more find itself reduced to a sexual commerce than the activity of polemarch or monarch can be compared to "human affairs," as understood by Clausewitz, for example.

The "to conquer is to advance" of Frederick II. Alexander's great haste in plunging ahead, thinking only of finding a limit to the indefinite expansion of his force of penetration, but also the driver's glance thrown at the speedometer of a racing car or military vehicle, as an existential measure of the being of the warrior, the vertiginous flow of time—perpetual assaults on distance also endlessly reproduce the original rite-of-passage, a résumé of the universe realized by the speed of the assault.

"Love is most often a by-product of murder," the novelist Christie liked to point out. From this Célinesque character who is constantly showing the remains of her children or of her husband, dead in the war, to the widows who inhabit their mourning like it was a situation of privilege, no longer leaving their homes, nourishing a scarcely disguised hatred at those who are still there, the survivors, and in particular their own progeny, to the Telegram: "If the war is lost let the nation perish!" in which Hitler decided to join his efforts with those of his enemy-partners in achieving the destruction of his own people by annihilating the last resources of their land—here we are not at the opposite but rather at the delirious apogee of seductive activity, moving in a world of absolute fatality where nothing makes sense, neither the good, nor bad, nor time, nor space; and where what others call success can no longer serve as criterion.[6]

The women of the Women's Liberation Movement develop similar attitudes in the end: they advertise their liberation like widows... "Cure Yourself of Love" is one of their slogans. They've killed the spouse, the father, the child, and these are themes that significantly created unanimity among them, abortion having, for example, a great force of symbolic overcoming, since it relates directly to the murder accomplished as a by-product of love. In the US all of this assumes the ultimate form of a new social struggle, without quarter, between clans who have again become openly homosexual, in the pursuit of power, money, influence.

In *The Taming of the Shrew*, Petruchio refuses his wife the services of a maid, proposing instead those of his master-at-arms: *My valet knows how to take care of my cuirasse, he'll have no trouble with your corset.* Through this absurd command, the deadly male already recognizes himself as his wife's past; his refulgent helmet, his fighting outfit, destined for the *rapprochement* of the homosexual duel, will soon be rendered useless, even harmful, by the inception of highly technical wars. In the 17th century there appeared in France some very strict rules about clothes, mandating that the male abandon the "right to beauty." But at the same time the wearing of the uniform became obligatory, in spite of the opposition of the nobility. The evolution of military equipment is obviously linked to that of the means of destruction, to the development of armament and to changes in maneuvers: the troop will soon no longer be the "theatrical troop" of the nobility, there are no longer leading roles, even if certain officers are still harboring their "formal wear" at the time of the attack that will see them effectively and definitively exit the scene. From uniformity we pass to invisibility as during the war of 1914 the authorities agree on the evident advantage in renouncing bright colors in the manufacture of uniforms and in adopting a habit of neutral shade to diminish the visibility of troops in the field. At war now there are only extras, masses of extras assembled to make a great number; after the color madder (red), too brilliant, they picked sky-blue, field-gray, gray-green and finally English army khaki, this color which is really much more than a color... the major concern being less with identification than disintegration, since the word comes from the Hindustani *khaki*, meaning color of dust. The disappearance of the body's characteristics in the uniformity of civil or military dress goes along with the disappearance of the body in the unidirectionality of speed. The abandoning of the right to beauty amounts to an entry into a new order of illusion. From now on, the strategic domain extends to the very rhythm of the different disappearances, the vehicles, troops, infrastructures, cities overexposed to bombardments, entire continents nothing any longer escapes planification of destruction; it's the great blackout... Soon the tankdriver's or pilot's habit will be only underwear for the habitation. At the beginning of the century the architect Adolf Loos wrote the manifesto *Ornament and Crime*, in which he proclaimed the following law: *As culture develops ornament disappears from everyday objects.*

He rejoices at the greatness of our time that is no longer, he says, able to invent a new ornamentation, "for it's a waste to make ornaments of materials, money or human lives— that's the true evil, the crime we've no right to be complacent about. Culture's progress resembles *the march of an army*— which would mean that most people would be laggards. It may be that I live in the year 1913. But one of my neighbors lives in 1900 and another in 1880... The peasant of the high valleys of the Tyrol lives in the 12th century... Happy the land that has neither marauders nor laggards! Only America can claim to be such a country. Even in our greatest cities we have the tardy, the retarded..."

At the beginning of the 20th century the woman progressively abandons her right to beauty, she quits her famous corset at a moment when the armament of the racer and the race for arms become social phenomena; the liberation of women liberates the seductions of technique. She can go for sports records, climb aboard fast machines; for her, also, the new corset-armature is a plane or automobile cockpit the attraction of the woman as by-product of murder or vector of voyage becomes null, the coupling yoke is broken and the only use of the feminine artifact is to enhance the value of the vehicle, in beauty parades, advertising metaphors and political or military propaganda. Woman has become one of those ornaments of older or exotic cultures that modern man employs or renounces as it suits him, not inventing new uses for her, for, as Adolf Loos remarks, *he reserves and concentrates his inventive faculties for other purposes.*

The disappearance of the woman in the fatality of the technical object creates a new mass language, a faithful reflection of the fascist language of the old futurist elite of the beginning of the century, "the heat of a piece of iron or wood is, from now on, more exciting for us than a woman's smile or tears... well transform into keen joy Edgar Poe's nevermore... with us commences the reign of rootless man, amplified man, alloyed with iron and feeding off electricity... This is tantamount to saying how very much we scorn propaganda for beautification of the landscape... and the great symbolists leaning over the naked body of the woman, woman-beauty, ideal and fatal" (Marinetti, 1910).

The pilot Jean-Marie Saget declared recently in an interview with *France Soir*: "At that time being a test pilot meant really *flying into the unknown*... but now we've got to deal with another frustration; it's a pity, but we can't fly the planes of competing companies because of the commercial competition. *I've never taken off in an F15*, I'm sorry to say. The company pilots, on the other hand, fly everything, because they've got to be able to make comparisons... they're privileged characters." At the moment of leaving and climbing into his Mirage 4000, Saget adds as a kind of goodbye: *I'm going to the other side!*

There really is a technological donjuanism, a hijacking of machines that renews that of logistical spouses. The former triangle is completely modified and the rapport is established between a *unisex* (definitive dissimulation of physiological identities) and a technical vector, contact with the body of the loved one or of the territorial body disappearing usually as the dynamics of the passage intensify.

However the assumption of the rites-of-passage by mass production is, we've seen, important for other reasons, since we can think, paraphrasing Rageot, that the entirety of technological civilization has finally applied itself only in *establishing in displacement the fixity of life*. "*Mobilis in mobili,*" mobile in the mobile, the motto of the *Nautilus* precedes the *you don't have speed, you are speed*, demonstrating in the quest for progress something which would no longer be discontinuous, a final abolition of differences, of distinctions between nature and culture, utopia and reality, since technology, in making the rite-of-passage a continuous phenomenon, would make of the derangement of the senses a permanent state, conscious life becoming an oscillating trip whose only absolute poles would be birth and death; and all this would mean, of course, the end of religions and philosophies.

Science would have effectively fabricated a new society whose members would have all become sleepers, living illusory days and naturally very much at ease in a situation of total peace, of nuclear dissuasion, the latter developing itself according to the principle of least resistance so dear to engineers: according to a curve of optimal distribution of the exertions of forces that guarantees their equilibrium and avoids accidents, a world utterly suspended on the threshold of a final operation that would realize effectively for humanity a rite-of-passage comparable to that of *Genesis* in its definitive fatality.

When, at the beginning of the century, Spengler predicted the *"return of science to its psychic homeland* and imminent ruin of Faustian civilization: its debris scattered here and there, railroads and passenger liners forgotten, as fossilized as the Roman roads or Chinese Wall..." he had no idea that these events, recent or ancient, were all larvae of speed, abandoned sketches of the West's unique and irresistable project and projection toward a technical beyond, finally as mysterious as that of the old religions, affronting the great natural events with the help of their special effects.

"If it's working, it's already obsolete!"—that is the paradox of the West, which we haven't sufficiently pondered, and which became Lord Mountbatten's motto during the last war, when he directed British weaponry research. It concerned the struggle, the competition between various war machines made by the belligerents. If a weapon works it will no longer be a "surprise" for the adversary and so will lose its efficacy, that is, its controlling quality as *accident.* But as always in the technical domain, war is the best model. The machine, because it was brought into the world, is no longer absent; it works. However, at the instant of its functioning it is no longer what is to come, it is obsolete—from which we derive the need for speed records; the record will link the technical machine with an imaginary dimension that is boundless— because no one can know the upper limits of speed.

We are currently rediscovering the mystery of the technical motor, we apprehend it less now as an object of consumption susceptible of being desired or rejected than as a strange processional accompaniment, outside of history, scarcely even geographic, a play of representations of the Self close to a dreamlike false day... *this delirious joy of speed that transcends the infinity of dreams* (Marinetti).

Around 1900 Colonel Rochas, former Director of Poly-technic, aimed to show with his xenoglossy "that a subject under hypnosis could exceed the limit of prior human experience and reascend time without too much effort..." The members of the "Crushing Automobile Club of the fifties"[7] gave themselves over to a comparable activity, but here the medium is no longer a woman, but American cars of the fifties, Cadillac, Buick, Ford, Chevrolet...

"Albert lives 1950 to the limit," a journalist writes on this subject, "during the week he drives an ordinary car, but when he takes out his Bel Air, he dresses as a Teddy Boy, his wife in the back seat with the kid, the way it was done at the time... *He had been dreaming about that car ever since he was fifteen years old.* As soon as he saw it he imagined it in its original color, shiny blue with the roof a bit paler, with lots of chrome, and looking like a rocket up front... 'At night,' Albert adds, 'I look at it. Before pulling it out of the garage I tap it on the side, I talk to it, you see, and when I added its rocket-front I felt that it needed it. You should see it in the evening, at twilight, as it vibrates, radiates, it's sensitive, a real nice heap'."

And there's Daniel (16 years old, second in his class, electromechanics), who declared to a journalist of *Le Monde*, concerning a car he was coveting: "I wanted a motorcycle, a big one, a very big one, to go far, where I want, *no matter where*. I wanted to go forever without ever stopping. I wanted it to be the one who drives when I'm tired. I wanted it to be like a boat, ocean blue, with distant sails, gulls flying around; or glistening with lights and chrome, illuminating everything suddenly; I wanted it to consume nothing, just a little bit of air, once in a while, and *I'd want it very fast so as to see only what I like*... I'd put in plenty of dials so that it could see me as well as I see it... I've got to tell you now what she's called: *I love you*..."

The machine completely replaces the loved one, the "mother land" inhabited by the spirit of metamorphosis, but technical fatality seems even more blinding and redoubtable than its anthropomorphic blueprints because of the very speed only it can lend to our aspirations. What is bought with the speed machine is no longer even the chance of the voyage but the surprise of the accident, which thousands of motorcyclists look for on the pirate course at Rungis every Saturday night, expecting it in the endless rounds they make. Dominique Pignon, physician, remarked about the Harrisburg nuclear reactor catastrophe:

"The *reality of the reactor*, as with everything that relates to the atom, cannot be captured in ordinary language... the most powerful computer is infinitely slow compared to real processes, and also in nuclear milieu experts know they are incapable of following on a computer what's really happening in a reactor that's out of control... in the event of an accident, then, they're like blind men turning round trying to make a decision."[8]

The technician becomes the victim of the movement he's produced; having become aphasic, he rehearses, in the absolute of the control room of the nuclear center, the simplified gestures of a primal magnetic rite whose "mobile-without-mobility" no one bothers to clarify.

He may remind us, from now on, of Captain Hatteras, Jules Verne's hero, a precursor of such real heroes as the Norwegian Roald Amundsen and the Italian Umberto Nobile, rushing into a beyond without an identity since it resembles nothing, while not being nothingness either: the North Pole, a sidereal desert. Nothing is vaster than empty things, said Bacon. To search, to seek out, to discover; but here all partners have definitively disappeared and Captain Hatteras, *this sad victim of a sublime passion*, has been afflicted with what his asylum doctor calls a polar folly... he's become one with a rite-of-passage toward the Septentrion.

"Followed by his faithful dog who watched him with soft and sad eyes, Captain Hatteras went out for long walks every day; but his walk was accomplished invariably according to an established pattern and in the direction of a certain path of Sten-Cottage. Once he got to the end of the path the Captain would start walking backwards. Had someone stopped him? He pointed to a fixed point in the sky... The doctor soon understood the motive force of this singular stubbornness, he guessed why this walk was always taken in the same direction, as if under the influence of a magnetic force. Captain John Hatteras walked invariably toward the north."[9]

4

The hurried man of Paul Morand is astounded by a cinematographic slow motion of a plane accident: "The plane grazes the ground, which then opens the plane up more delicately than a gourmet peels his fig..."; the most violent, murderous shock seems as sweet as a sequence of kisses. We've since improved on this visual impression by producing collisions experimentally, populating them with cadavers, filming them at different speeds and with the help of various cameras.[1]

After man's walking, then his dancing, what's given over to film is the slow choreography associating dead bodies with vehicular motion, a sort of amorous revelation for the couple formed by technophilia and speed, *which in telescoping two caresses makes for a mortal mess.*

The cinematic motor has accustomed us to finding the mystery of movement in this transitory world natural, to no longer wonder how acceleration of amorous gesture can suddenly become murderous, how the Pavan dance of a falling or propelled body can become fatal. At the same time this vulgarized violence of movement, revealed by the distortion of vision, shows us its inconsistency; the violence of speed dominates the technical world but remains nevertheless, as in the time of the Sphinx, the basic enigma.

When Mountbatten was assassinated, in the month of August 1979, a witness, Brian Wakely, recounts: "There was a boat—there—and suddenly there is nothing. I was on a dinghy that Mountbatten's boat had just grazed. I heard the noise of the explosion only after seeing it blown to bits!"

This feeling of supernatural strangeness, we experienced it, for example, during the bombardments of the last war: the explosion in sheaves of flowers and smoke of an artwork happening far away, but within eyesight and in total silence. The dust had already settled when we finally became aware of the noise of the explosion. Speed again ostensibly perverts the illusory order of normal perception, the order of arrival of information. What could have seemed simultaneous is diversified and decomposes. With speed, the world keeps on coming at us, to the detriment of the object, which is itself now assimilated to the sending of information. It is this intervention that destroys the world as we know it, technique finally reproducing permanently the violence of the accident; the mystery of speed remains a secret of light and heat from which even sound is missing.

The techniques of rationality have ceaselessly distanced us from what we've taken as the advent of an objective world: the rapid tour, the accelerated transport of people, signs or things, reproduce—by aggravating them—the effects of picnolepsy, since they provoke a perpetually repeated hijacking of the subject from any spatial-temporal context.

From the very inception of the transportation revolution certain persons had the merit of discerning in the desire for movement, peregrination, voyage, more of a desire for the discovery of speed than any far-off elsewhere.

In 1903 Bierbaum declaims against this tendency: "Speed is not the goal!" He himself is searching for what he calls a *humanist speed* without which, he warns, "we would be embarking on a 'carriage of fools' (*Narrenkutsche*) that takes the place of the Ship of Fools; speed must become a particular cultural aspect that serves collective culture."

But what, exactly, does culture as we understand it here, have to do with the kind of kicks sought by characters such as d'Annunzio or Georg Müller, who affirm that vehicular speed "allows us to think of nothing, to feel nothing, to attain indifference"; we might say that this anchoritic speed is literally the end of bourgeois culture, the reaction against exoticism and the lyricism of the voyage, "this Baroque beyond that has been in style since the end of the 18th and beginning of the 19th centuries with the first railroads."[2]

From the very beginning the search for high speeds was combined with destructive games of war and hunting, creators of elites. This is how war has been transformed from tedious work, where the elites were only servants of the weapons systems, into a more comfortable instrument, under the influence of the engineers, an indolence (Vauban). The exploitation of high speeds naturally becomes a sport reserved for dandy-warriors, a fantasy allowed to people who are otherwise useless, a new form of idleness permitted the well-to-do, which will make them regard movement itself as a life-style, "combining risk and comfort," said Marshall Goering, himself a drug addict and notorious dandy. From now on the traveler, in peopling the modes of rapid transport, becomes a negator of terrestrial dimensions.

Around 1920 Rageot writes: "Today's traveler can say: I am an inhabitant of earth, just as if he were saying: I am an inhabitant of Asnières... There are travelers who no longer even know they're traveling."

Endosmosis of the living being produced by technical acceleration; Craig Breedlove, holder of the world land speed record in 1965, entitles the preface to a book of memories: "*Doing something other than merely living*," and he notes: "Why does man aspire to these terrifying speeds, entering a wheeled vehicle powerful enough not only to carry him off to glory but also to tear him to pieces?"

If all is movement all is at the same time accident and our existence as metabolic vehicle can be summed up as a series of collisions, of traumatisms, some taking on the quality of slow but perceptible caresses; but all this, according to the impulsions lent them, becomes mortal shocks and apotheoses of fire, but above all *a different mode of being*. Speed is a cause of death for which we're not only responsible but of which we are also the creators and inventors—so it's been said.

As a young man I wondered about the aesthetics of war machines, what I called in my inner sanctum their enigma. I found myself often contemplating a bunker or the silhouette of some submarine seen at a distance, wondering why their polished forms were so inscrutable and where did their kind of plastic invisibility come from?

At first I related this to zoomorphism, to metamorphism, but all of that was comparison, imitation and could not satisfy me. Then I believed these forms were inscrutable because they all related to speeds that were different, excessive, and thus fatally reflecting another image of the universe meant to fill up other times; they belonged to other worlds which are invisible to the naked eye, yet something of which remained with them. But the over-production of movement implied by war changed the way things looked; the motor, since it relates directly to the state of paradoxical wakefulness, replaced the causal idea—that was its revolution; *the motor proceeds from the soul.*

And so when the playful Méliès disguises himself as Satan of the operetta, doesn't he hit the nail right on the head: the tree of the motor is the tree of knowledge (science), corruption of sight is corruption of life!

In the last century we had already become aware of the paradox of speed: "The train doesn't make voyagers of us but packages that are expedited..." remarked Tolstoy. The hurried man of Morand ruminates: "We need to find something even more idiotic to block the course of time completely, total abstention from all action..." To say today that speed is obsolete is an untruth as obvious as that which consists in praising slowness. Hughes was already aping our technical future: the abandonment of the vehicular speed of bodies for the strangely impressive one of light vectors, the internment of bodies is no longer in the cinematic cell of travel but in a cell outside of time, which would be an electronic terminal where we'd leave it up to the instruments to organize our most intimate vital rhythms, without ever changing position ourselves, the authority of electronic automatism reducing our will to zero... somehow the vision of light moving on a screen would have replaced all personal movement.

"We can imagine for the future," writes Charles Schreider, "a transformation (of reality) into video signals stored on tape, or better yet *a decomposition and coding of images in digital signals capable of storage in various materials...*"

The development of high technical speeds would thus result in the disappearance of consciousness as the direct perception of phenomena that inform us of our own existence.

Technology introduces a phenomenon without precedent in the mediation of time, for if we've affirmed that time is only one reality, that of the instant, we might also say with Guyon, as the motor is being invented: "The idea of time can be reduced to a point of view: duration is made of transitory instants just as a straight line is made of points without depth."

Dimensions vanish in the reduction of straightness or of a straightaway, which would be only the speed of a geometric trajectory. The will to carry out whatever is possible, contained in diverse applications of the exact sciences, has led to a new atrophy of the instant, as essentially involving a before and an after. By introducing the subject into the hierarchy of speeds (lower, higher), by destabilizing the instant, a contingent phenomenon, the standards are abrogated; the diversifying of speed also abrogates the sensation of general duration, of continuous movement. Méliès understood early on that cinema is *not a seventh art but an art that combines all of the others*: drawing, painting, architecture, music, but also mechanical, electrical works, etc.

Cinema is the end in which the dominant philosophies and arts have come to confuse and lose themselves, a sort of primordial mixing of the human soul and the languages of the motor-soul. The chronology of the arts in history already demonstrates this decomposition: for example, at a concert the extreme emphasis on auditory attention annihilates any other body movement, revealing the basic connection between the musical instrument (a veritable sound motor with its cylinders, rhythms) and speed—properly the manna of every listener.

As Ribot writes in *The Psychology of Attention*: "Without the motor elements perception is impossible..." And R. Philip establishes, for example, a "measurement" of the listener's attention: "Music modifies the respiratory and cardiac rhythm which is slowed down or speeded up," as in visual attention, if associated with an obligatory eye movement, it is also linked to an inevitable inhibition of bodily movements.[3]

Shortly before his death, Nero, back in Naples, stopped to admire a new musical instrument, a water organ invented, according to Vitruvius, by Ctesibius of Alexandria: it looked like an elongated buffet covered with tubes. Nero's bright idea, then, is to play the organ while confronting his enemies, thinking he will thereby win them over. Nero's pretension is not so unrealistic: at a concert, when the musical motor shuts off, not only is there a liberating violence of ovations and handclapping but also a thunderstorm of sneezing, coughing, scraping of feet—as if everyone suddenly reacquired posses- sion of his own body. The very development of symphonic music ends up with the orchestra leader in the privileged position of *sole conductor*, but what he directs is not only the increasingly numerous musical troop but also the mass of auditors he's responsible for immobilizing in their chairs... to openly leave one's seat becomes here the most devastating of musical critiques!

Technician-culture has only extended this assumption of control by motor elements, steadily increasing our dependency on directional systems of accountability and control (speedometers, dashboards, remote tele-control). Initiating itineraries of direction, technician-culture applies to earth and nature (human nature) Bacon's formula: *Nothing is vaster than empty things...* creating finally emptiness and desert because only nothingness can be continuous, and therefore conductive.

Rather than trying for speed records in the vast celestial spaces, champions like Art Afrons declare that *the most exciting, exalting, dynamic task that exists consists in attempting intellec- tually, physically and technically the land speed record on our mother earth... a work of love*, he specifies, and the word does not seem unintended.

Likewise Malcolm Campbell, a former RAF pilot, sees sensations of flight as insipid and less intoxicating compared to those he tasted on land on board the various "blue-birds."

In fact, the passion for speed had seized him in early youth, writes Leo Villa, at the same time as the passion for those mysterious stories which always involved *hidden treasures waiting for the heroes able to unearth them.*

As an adult he was going to try to realize these several dreams.[4]

Therefore the earth (ground-effect) seems paradoxically to remain the privileged partner of the seeker of absolute records, to whom nevertheless she exposes the dangers of natural obstacles, gravity, etc., the speed record coming as much from the search for new technical blends as from that of planed, smoothed surfaces. The vastness of space is no longer sought except as a means of putting into question the experience of discontinuity. "Time and space seem infinite to us only when they don't exist," Roupnel suggested. The immediacy of terrestrial transport, modifying the relation to space, annihilates the relation to lived time and it's in this urgency that its dynamic exaltation consists. Paradoxically, it's the extreme mobility which creates the inertia of the moment, instantaneity which would create the instant! Finally the instant becomes like the illusory perception of a stability, clearly revealed by technical prostheses, such as is demonstrated for us by Einstein's example of passing trains: the feeling of the instant can only be given by coincidence (*epiteikos*), the moment when two trains seem immobile to travelers while they are really launched at top speed one beside the other. The notion of a time, which, according to Bachelard, would accommodate only the reality of the instant, could only be established on the basis of our remaining unconscious of our own speeds in a world entirely given over to the law of movement *and thereby the creator of the illusion of inertia.*

What creates the difference between the diverse intuitions of time is the position in space of the reasoning consciousness, a little like in Edgar Poe's allegory, *The Gold Bug*, where the seeker has to commit himself to numerous speculations on the cryptogramic significance of the message, before moving in any given direction.

This mobility of the synoptic trajectory, in modifying the subject's point-of-view, is going to allow him the discovery of what, somehow, was already visible. Beyond that one is led back ineluctably to the fascination of the shiny bug, which is initiatory in the sense that, as the perspective point on an horizon of speed, it reduces the rest of the world to nothing. Passing from the course to the finish line, technique has been applied to make of this modification of perspective the supreme goal that it's eager to reach. The motor creates an unprecedented movement toward what eludes everyone's view and understanding (the treasure), like a tale about unseen things, involving the kind of space and time of metaphysical entities deprived of all reality, that Gastineau wrote about in the 19th century.

The conquest of speed and the search for treasure blend together absolutely in the longings of Malcolm Campbell, while the heyday of utopian tales, in general, is that of far-off expeditions, of the Renaissance quest of the Golden Fleece or the bellicose romanticism of the 19th century.

Reconciliation of nothingness and reality, the annihilation of time and space by high speeds substitutes the vastness of emptiness for that of the exoticism of travel, which was obvious for people like Heine who saw in this very annihilation the supreme goal of technique.[5] A little later the maniacs of aerodynamics and land speed records articulate this also, considering as primordial the reaction of the milieu to the object's form-in-movement and vice-versa. Their purpose is to create time out of everything, a time that would no longer be one, where, as Breedlove writes, *one simply exists*, a time that would be on earth yet nowhere. In the science fiction film *Close Encounters of the Third Kind*, extraterrestrials, accustomed to circulating in the immensity of intergalactic space, are enormously pleased to be traveling on a simple highway. Meanwhile the earthlings are enjoying hugely the paradox of this relation between pleasure and violation of limits, an exaltation which resembles closely enough that of the mountain climber who doesn't want so much to scale the peak as level off and flatten the mountain.

Chevallier notices it also: from Egyptian antiquity on we have geography, but also *chorography*,[6] almost entirely neglected by the historian—a figure of the road-building surge of Empires, as distinct from the mere mapping out of its territory. In spite of the transportation revolution of the 19th century, our historical discourse has remained tied to a culture based on a common conception of space and time, while contemporaneously a new life style was being worked out, a cultural innovation consisting in a new reading of duration, if only in the plain example of the railroad, of its network schedules with their complex interconnections, unprecedented chorography that had to be made understandable for every traveler. There is no longer involved in this practice any rapport between a pretension to live one's own unique historical time and this manner of suddenly finding oneself in motion and in transit in railroad car compartments, that are also, for their user, compartments of space and time. The administration of transportation confirms Bachelard's observation: "After Einstein's relativity, metaphysics had to retreat to local time, everything having to do with the external proof of unique duration as a clear principle of ordination of events was ruined…" Einstein's theory completed the destruction of a Pharaonic conception of signs as immobile bodies immutably arrayed against the passing of time, capable of resurging in History, of resuscitating in the beyond… a conception that explains clearly enough the cult of mausoleums as well as doctrinaire survivals in Marxist countries, attached to the idea of a unique historical duration.

That the totalitarian European regimes would be hostile to Einstein's theories was also to be expected, since time with them appears less given than locally invented, and it was equally to be expected that Einstein, in spite of himself, be drawn into the tragic confrontation with total war, which in 1939 became the war of time(s).

However, in this new kind of conflict, it is already no longer a matter of local times; the history of battles revealed de-localization as precipitation toward an ultimate metaphysical record, a final oblivion of matter and of our own presence in the world, beyond the barrier of sound and soon of light.

Notes

PART 1

1. See Catherine Bousquet's text and bibliography in *Macroscopies* 6, p. 45. "Epilepsy—*surprise* in Greek—assumes not only one form but several and we have to speak of epilepsies, from the *Grand Mal* to the *Petit Mal*. From the neurological point of view all epileptic crises result, strictly speaking, from a hyper-synchronous discharge of a population of neurons ... The clinical way of conceiving epilepsy has changed very little over the years, except that we now distinguish the epileptic attack from epilepsy properly speaking, reserving the term rather for chronic crises."

2. From the Latin *discurrere*, to run here and there, a term that very well conveys the impression of haste and disturbance of normal mental operations in the picnoleptic.

3. "Hysteria and epilepsy, specifically feminine maladies ... Sensitive, sentimental women, great readers of novels, expert in the games of coquettry ..." (Regnard).

4. See Benoît Mandelbrot. *Les Objets Fractals* (*The Fractal Objects*). Paris: Flammarion, 1975. Through the constant renewal of the relations between the semblance and the mobile, occidental geometry would have proceeded to a regulation of diverse forms of representation: "As confirmation, let's demonstrate that a complex object, for instance a spool 10 cm. in diameter, made of thread 1 mm wide, possesses in some fashion, latently, several distinct physical dimensions ..."

5. See bibliography and bio-filmography by Geroges Sadol. *Georges Méliès*. Paris: Seghers, 1961.

6. *E.J. Marey, 1830–1904.* Qtd. in a monograph for the 1977 exhibition at the Georges Pompidou Center, Paris. "The mechanism of our normal consciousness is of a cinematic nature," notes Bergson, who knew Marey.

7. See Shmuel Trigano. "Midbar, Chemama." *Traverses* 19 (June 1980). See also Paul Virilio. *L'Insécurité du territoire* (*The Insecurity of Territory*). Paris: Stock, 1975. "The State is always the court, the city (Urstaat) ..."

8. See Jean Duvignaud. *Le jeu du jeu* (*The Game of the Game*). Paris: Balland, 1980.

9. As in Bernstein's joke: "Intuition is intelligence that is speeding!" You might think of a certain restitution of ethnological definitions: soul, manna, potential substance, breath and energy, etc.

10. The fundamental elements of speed, of childhood, of power over destiny, are already assembled here. With Orson Welles, as with many Anglo-Saxons, *the presence of absence* is a major theme.

11. James Phelan. *Howard Hughes*. Montréal: Alain Stanké International Editions, 1977.

12. See Paul Virilio. *L'Insécurité du territoire* (*The Insecurity of Territory*). Paris: Stock, 1975, p. 171. "The human space becoming that of no one becomes progression of nowhere ..."

13. G.E.R. Lloyd. *Magic, Reason and Experience*. Oxford: Cambridge University Press, 1979. See also *Les débuts de la science grecque. De Thales à Aristote* (*Early Greek Science: Thales to Aristotle*). Paris: Éditions Maspero, 1974.

14. Claude Bernard, a methodical thinker whose disciple Marey was, notes the order of scientific work: feeling first, then reason and experience. See *Introduction à l'étude de la médecine expérimentale*. Paris: 1865.

15. See Perniola, Mario. "Logique de la séduction" ("The Logic of Seduction"). *Traverses* 18 (February 1980).

PART 2

1. New York: Semiotext(e), 1977; rpt. 2007. "The State's political power, therefore, is only secondarily 'power organized by one class to oppress another.' More materially, *it is the polis, the police, in other words highway surveillance*."

2. See Alain Jaubert. "Electrochocs" ("Electroschock"). *Macroscopies* 6, p. 28.

3. See Aldous Huxley. *L'Art de voir*. Paris: Petite Bibliothèque Payot, 1978. Original publication: Aldous Huxley. *The Art of Seing*, New York and London: Harper

& Brothers Publishers, 1942. "Almost blind since he was 16, Huxley had very bad vision until 1939, when he discovered Doctor Bates' method of visual re-education, which allowed him in a few months to read without glasses. Subsequently he wrote *The Art of Seeing*, where he explained these methods."

4. The singer Claude François utilized comparable methods for the music hall. He always made himself up, from the beginning, before an enlarging mirror surrounded by candles: their changing light was a perfect prelude, according to him, for the light of the stage. Furthermore he combined the extreme sadness of his songs with light and joyous music and dancing.

5. See Virilio, Paul. *La Dromoscopie ou la lumiere de la vitesse* (*Dromoscopy, or the Speed of Light*). Paris: Éditions de Minuit, 1978.

6. Gaston Rageot. *L'Homme standard* (*The Standard Man*). Paris: Librairie Plon, 1928. Ten years later, Morand, inspired by this book, wrote *L'Homme pressé* (*The Hurried Man*).

7. Pierre Souvestre and Marcel Allain. *Fantômas—Un roi prisonnier* (*Fantomas: A Royal Prisoner*). Paris: Editions Laffont, 1961.

8. Gaston Rageot.

9. See the series of articles by Jacqueline Cartier, "Mickey au pays des merveilles" ("Mickey in Wonderland"), published in *France Soir*, January 1979. The phenakistoscope, in effect, takes on the form of a carousel; the turning machine gives the illusion of movement by the persistence of optical sensations (from the *Greek: phenax + akos, deceitful*, and *skopein*, examine).

10. "*Yom*, the Hebrew day which began at twilight, exile of light, exodus from Ur … The Hebrew day is between two lights!" (Shmuel Trigano). The day-without-twilight of the polemarch is directly opposed to the Biblical day.

11. "We'd rather be happy entirely for a day than experience half-happiness for a week," writes Marshal Richelieu. Saint-Just is not far! As Flaubert claims, the essential thing in a work is its unity. For him this unity consists in a dominant coloration and he explains that, in writing *Madame Bovary*, he intended to render a single tone, near-white, as indefinable as the color of moisture. Finally, a controlling light in which diversity of colors is lost. But European painting has always pretended to the photogenic illusion, diffusing light while previous methods had only received it. You can find here the basis for the allusion of Bradbury to "Rembrandt and Disney"!

PART 3

1. See Lawrence Leshan. *The Medium, the Mystic and the Physicist—Toward a General Theory of the Paranormal.* New York: Viking Press, 1974.

2. The serpent serving as a mask to a hostile being in which Wisdom, then Christianity, wanted to recognize Satan. "The woman saw that the fruit of the tree of knowledge was good to eat and pleasing to look upon …"

3. The man *âdam* comes from the earth, *adâma.* "Garden" is translated "paradise" in the Greek version. Eden is a geographical name that can't be tied down to any particular place; it might first have meant "steppe." See "Commentary" in *La Bible de Jérusalem* (*The Jerusalem Bible*). Paris: Les Editions du Cerf, 1961.

4. See *Equicola* 95, and Anthony Blunt. *Artistic Theory in Italy, 1450–1600.* Oxford: Oxford University Press, 1962. "There is always a difference between the 'liberal' and the 'automatic,' which is pure motor movement, a mechanical matter which can be performed equally well by the ignorant or by animals."
Couldn't find date into for Equicola.

5. "If you have no wife, go into the bush, follow a mare and make her your wife" (Dogon proverb). "Man is woman's passenger, not only at birth, but also during sexual relations … you might say that the female is the means man has chosen to reproduce himself, that is to say to come to the world." Paul Virilio. "Metempsychose du passager." *Traverses* 8 (May 1977).

6. The separation between genitors and progeny has been constantly growing due to the drift of legal opinion. If the law of 1968 on adoption allows the alteration of the infant's civil status, whose real name is erased from the register, the 2,000 babies born in France through artificial insemination remain without any true legal status.

7. See an interesting text in *Libération* by Corinne Brisedou, on collectors of fifties cars and their nocturnal meetings the first Friday of every month at Place de la Concorde, Paris.

8. Dominique Pignon. *Des Risques d'accident dans in centrales nucléaires* (*The Risk of Accidents in Nucleur Power Plants*). Paris: Christian Bourgois, eds, 1975.

9. Verne, Jules. *Les Aventures du capitaine Hatteras: Les Anglais au pôle Nord—Le désert de glace* (*The Adventures of Captain Hatteras: The English at the North Pole—The Desert of Ice*). Paris: Hachette, 1966.

PART 4

1. "Special models" (S.M.) are human bodies, fresh and in good condition, used by Renault for research into automobile safety. A thousand S.M. have been used in the last few years at the Landy Center, in the Paris region.

2. Claube Pichois. *Vitesse et vision du monde* (*Speed and Vision of the World*). Neuchâtel: Éditions de la Baconnière, 1973.

3. Aldous Huxley. *The Art of Seing*, New York and London: Harper & Brothers Publishers, 1942.

4. See Leo Villa. *Les Tombeurs de records* (*The Record Breakers*). Paris: Hatier, 1972. "Constant observer for 45 years, the Campbell's mechanic, Leo Villa, says that for the father as well as the son the only thing that counted was being the fastest man in the world. Donald Campbell, going over 444 km/h aboard his jet powered speedboat, disintegrated in an explosion in January 1967."

5. See Heinrich Heine. *Lutèce*. Paris: Éditions Michel Levy Frères, 1855. "Through the railroads space has been abolished and the only thing left for us is time …"

6. Raymond Chevallier. *Les Voies romaines* (*The Roman Roads*). Paris: Librairie Armand Cohn, 1972. "We expected to find, notably in their historians, precise information about the construction of roads, the basis for Roman power. None of that information exists, history in Rome being, above all, political and psychological …"